ACE® PERSONAL TRAINER MANUAL
STUDY COMPANION

FIFTH EDITION

ACE®
AMERICAN COUNCIL ON EXERCISE

4851 Paramount Drive | San Diego, California 92123 | 800-825-3636 | ACEfitness.org

F G H I

Distributed by:
American Council on Exercise
4851 Paramount Drive
San Diego, CA 92123
(858) 576-6500
(858) 576-6564 FAX
ACEfitness.org

Project Editor: Daniel J. Green
Technical Editors: Cedric X. Bryant, Ph.D., FACSM, & Sabrena Jo, M.S.
Art Direction: Karen McGuire
Production: Nancy Garcia

P17-009

TABLE OF CONTENTS

STUDYING FOR THE ACE PERSONAL TRAINER EXAM

WELCOME TO THE *ACE PERSONAL TRAINER MANUAL STUDY COMPANION*, A GUIDE designed to complement the *ACE Personal Trainer Manual* (5th Edition). The exercises in this book will help you learn the basics of personal training by breaking them into manageable concepts that you can apply to real-life situations.

The most important study tool you will utilize is the *ACE Personal Trainer Manual* (5th Edition). This book, the *ACE Personal Trainer Manual Study Companion*, contains helpful, multiple-choice questions for each corresponding chapter of the *ACE Personal Trainer Manual* as well as a summary review of each chapter that will help you focus your studies.

ACE's Essentials of Exercise Science for Fitness Professionals and that text's corresponding flashcards are valuable reference materials that contain their own specific multiple-choice questions.

This study companion corresponds only with the *ACE Personal Trainer Manual* (5th Edition).

HOW TO USE YOUR STUDY COMPANION

1. After reading chapters in the *ACE Personal Trainer Manual* (5th Edition), carefully review topics from the Summary Review of each corresponding chapter of the *ACE Personal Trainer Manual Study Companion*. This content highlights valuable information that is relevant to fitness professionals, both in importance and frequency of application or occurrence in the practice of personal training.

2. Next, answer the Chapter Review Questions.

3. Finally, check your answers using the corresponding Answer Key. Review the section in the *ACE Personal Trainer Manual* (5th Edition) associated with any questions you may have missed.

IMPORTANT TIPS

- To register for your exam, do not forget that you must hold a current certificate in cardiopulmonary resuscitation (CPR) and, if living in North America, proper use of an automated external defibrillator (AED). The course must be completed as a live course that you attend in person; an online certificate course is not accepted. As you begin your studies, start looking into local providers and register for a course.

- As you make your way through all of the material, be sure to keep an eye out for the "Key Concepts," which highlight essential information you will need to understand as you prepare for the ACE exam. In addition, pay special attention to the boldface terms in the chapters, which are defined in the glossary.

- As a general rule, ACE recommends that candidates allow approximately three to four months of study time on average to adequately prepare for the ACE Personal Trainer Certification Exam.

- For additional tips and resources, check out the Study Center Facebook page at Facebook.com/ACEfitnessStudyCenter and the Exam Preparation Blog at www.ACEfitness.org/blogs/2/exam-preparation-blog.

  If you have additional questions, contact ACE at support@acefitness.org or (888) 825-3636.

ROLE AND SCOPE OF PRACTICE FOR THE
PERSONAL TRAINER

READING ASSIGNMENT

You should now have completed the reading of Chapter 1 of the *ACE Personal Trainer Manual,* 5th Edition. Carefully review the Summary Review below, as this content highlights valuable information that is particularly relevant to fitness professionals, both in importance and frequency of application or occurrence in the practice of personal training.

Then, answer the Chapter 1 Review Questions and check your answers using the corresponding Answer Key. Review the section in the *ACE Personal Trainer Manual,* 5th Edition, associated with any questions you may have missed.

SUMMARY REVIEW

Personal trainers must be prepared to work with clients ranging in age from youth to older adults, and ranging in health and fitness status from overweight and sedentary to athletic.

Personal trainers should have a solid understanding of the research linking physical activity to health, as well as knowledge of guidelines for physical activity, such as the *2008 Physical Activity Guidelines for Americans* developed by the U.S. Department of Health & Human Services.

THE ALLIED HEALTHCARE CONTINUUM

Personal trainers should understand the roles of the professionals in the following specialty areas within allied healthcare, as well as the role of fitness professionals in relation to other members of the healthcare team:

- Physicians/nurse practitioners
- Rehabilitation professionals
- Nutritional support
- Mental health practitioners
- Alternative healthcare (licensed) professionals
- Trainers/coaches/instructors

THE ACE PERSONAL TRAINER CERTIFICATION

A qualified and effective ACE Certified Personal Trainer has an understanding of the following concepts:

- Definition of "scope of practice"
- Scope of practice for ACE Certified Personal Trainers
- Knowledge, skills, and abilities of the ACE Certified Personal Trainer
- Education and experience required to service clients
- Preparation recommendations and testing requirements for sitting for the ACE Personal Trainer Exam Certification
- Professional responsibilities and ethics
  - ✓ ACE Code of Ethics
  - ✓ ACE Professional Practices and Disciplinary Procedures

✓ Certification period and renewal
✓ Client privacy
✓ Referral
✓ Safety
✓ Supplements and other nutrition-related concerns
✓ Ramifications of offering services outside the scope of practice

ACCREDITATION OF ALLIED HEALTHCARE CREDENTIALS

The ACE Certified Personal Trainer should understand the importance of third-party accreditation from a credible organization like the National Commission for Certifying Agencies, as well as the following concepts related to the advancement of personal training within the allied healthcare environment:

- Recognition from the fitness and health industry
- Recognition from the education community
- Recognition from the department of labor

CAREER DEVELOPMENT

Every personal trainer should have a general idea of the career path that he or she wants to follow. After setting a career plan, a personal trainer can use it as a template for researching and selecting continuing education to work toward his or her goals by understanding the opportunities available in the following areas:

- Continuing education
  ✓ Advanced knowledge
  ✓ Specialization
- Degrees
- Additional fitness certifications
- New areas of expertise within allied healthcare

GETTING STARTED

This chapter introduces the role of the ACE Certified Personal Trainer within the healthcare community and provides guidelines for staying within the defined scope of practice. This chapter also covers safety concerns in a fitness facility, as well as consultation and privacy issues. After completing this chapter, you will have a better understanding of:

- The knowledge, skills, and abilities associated with being a successful personal trainer
- The ACE Code of Ethics
- ACE's Professional Practices and Disciplinary Procedures
- How the ACE certification has received recognition from the fitness and health industry, the education community, and the department of labor
- The importance of a career-development plan

REVIEW QUESTIONS

1. The **PRIMARY** purpose of professional certifications is to

   _____.

   A. Provide the professional with additional education to enhance his or her knowledge, skills, and abilities

   B. Enhance a professional's resume for employment and/or higher compensation

   C. Protect the public from harm by assessing if candidates meet established levels of minimum competence

   D. Confirm a candidate's understanding of key concepts following the completion of a bachelor's degree

2. Which of the following is **WITHIN** the scope of practice for personal trainers?

   A. Counseling clients through life experiences that negatively impact program adherence

   B. Screening clients for exercise limitations to facilitate exercise program design

   C. Evaluating client injuries while designing rehabilitative exercise programs

   D. Recommending effective supplements for clients who skip meals

3. Which of the following is **OUTSIDE** the ACE Certified Personal Trainer scope of practice?

   A. Developing exercise programs for clients who have type 2 diabetes and medical clearance for exercise

   B. Providing guidance, motivation, and feedback to empower individuals to adhere to their exercise programs

   C. Implementing post-rehabilitative exercise programs for clients following their physicians' recommendations

   D. Compiling detailed nutritional programming and specific meal planning recommended by their physician

4. At what point does a candidate for the ACE Personal Trainer Certification (or any other ACE certification) agree to uphold the ACE Code of Ethics?

   A. While registering for an ACE certification exam

   B. Once the candidate earns his or her first ACE certification

   C. Upon receiving a printed copy of the ACE Code of Ethics with the printed ACE certification

   D. When accepting his or her first job as an ACE Certified Personal Trainer

5. ACE Certified Personal Trainers must complete a minimum of 20 hours of continuing education every two years to maintain their certifications. The **PRIMARY** reason ACE has established this minimum continuing-education requirement is to help ACE Certified Personal Trainers _____.

   A. Earn promotions so they can advance their careers

   B. Increase their earning potential by adding new specialty certificates to their résumés

   C. Enhance their résumés to attract more clients

   D. Stay current with the latest exercise science research and guidelines for fitness and health

6. Which of the following is **WITHIN** the ACE Certified Personal Trainer scope of practice?

   A. Helping clients gain a better understanding of portion sizes and healthful foods so they can make better choices

   B. Providing clients with recipes and shopping lists for four weeks to get them on track with healthful eating

   C. Conducting 24-hour dietary recalls to help clients learn where they have micronutrient deficiencies

   D. Educating clients about resting metabolic rate (RMR) and the need to consume fewer calories than RMR to lose weight

7. A personal trainer who wants to provide massage to help clients who have tight or sore muscles can do so **ONLY** if

   _____.

   A. The personal trainer has extensive knowledge about the benefits of massage

   B. The client gives his or her consent for the massage

   C. The personal trainer becomes a licensed massage therapist

   D. The massage therapist is not available and the personal trainer has some training

8. What do most allied health certification programs, such as the credentials for registered dietitians, occupational therapists, and nurse practitioners, have in common with certifications from the American Council on Exercise?

   A. They require a bachelor's degree as a minimum eligibility requirement

   B. They are accredited by the National Commission for Certifying Agencies

   C. They share the same collective scope of practice in allied health

   D. They meet the competency-based exam requirement for licensure in most states.

9. Which of the following is **MOST** accurate regarding personal trainers recommending supplements to their clients?

   A. The personal trainer should only recommend those supplements covered under his or her professional liability insurance.

   B. Unless the personal trainer has other credentials such as an R.D. or M.D., he or she does not possess the qualifications to legally recommend supplements.

   C. The personal trainer should become educated about the specific supplements before making any recommendations.

   D. Due to potential complications from taking supplements with other medications, personal trainers should recommend only plant-based supplements.

10. ACE Certified Personal Trainers looking to advance their knowledge, skills, and abilities beyond their ACE Personal Trainer Certification would be **BEST** served by completing what type of continuing education?

    A. A second NCCA-accredited personal-trainer certification

    B. A workshop that focuses on how to incorporate supplementation into a nutrition plan

    C. An online personal-training certification from an organization that is not NCCA-accredited

    D. An advanced fitness certification that is NCCA-accredited

11. As a general rule, ACE recommends that candidates allow _____ of study time to adequately prepare for the ACE Personal Trainer Certification Exam.

    A. 1 to 2 months

    B. 3 to 4 months

    C. 5 to 6 months

    D. 7 to 8 months

ANSWER KEY

1. C. Protect the public from harm by assessing if the candidates meet established levels of minimum competence

The primary purpose of a certification is always to protect the public from harm by assessing if the professional meets established levels of competence in the knowledge, skills, and abilities necessary to perform the job in a safe and effective manner.
ACE Personal Trainer Manual, 5th Edition, p. 7

2. B. Screening clients for exercise limitations to facilitate exercise program design

Personal trainers screen clients, design exercise programs, coach, and refer to more qualified members of the healthcare continuum as necessary. Fitness professionals do not "counsel," "rehabilitate," or recommend supplements to clients.
ACE Personal Trainer Manual, 5th Edition, p. 9–10

3. D. Compiling detailed nutritional programming and specific meal planning recommended by their physician

Personal trainers can show clients how to utilize the tools available at www.ChooseMyPlate.gov or educating them about the recommendations in the *Dietary Guidelines*. Clients looking for more detailed nutritional programming, such as specific meal plans, recipes, or recommendations for nutritional supplements, should be referred to a registered dietitian.
ACE Personal Trainer Manual, 5th Edition, p. 8–9

4. A. While registering for an ACE certification exam

Every individual who registers for an ACE certification exam must agree to uphold the ACE Code of Ethics throughout the exam process and as a professional, should he or she earn an ACE certification. Exam candidates and ACE Certified Personal Trainers must have a comprehensive understanding of the code and the consequences and potential public harm that can come from violating each of its principles.
ACE Personal Trainer Manual, 5th Edition, p. 13

5. D. Stay current with the latest exercise science research and guidelines for fitness and health

Continuing education is a standard requirement in healthcare to help ensure that professionals stay up-to-date with the latest research in their respective fields for the protection of the public. By completing continuing education, ACE Certified

Professionals can stay current with the latest findings in exercise science and keep their services in line with the most recent guidelines for fitness and healthcare.
ACE Personal Trainer Manual, 5th Edition, p. 13–14

6. A. Helping clients gain a better understanding of portion sizes and healthful foods so they can make better choices

Personal Trainers can show clients how to utilize the tools available at www.ChooseMyPlate.gov or educating them about the recommendations in the *Dietary Guidelines* to help them gain a better understanding of healthful foods and make better choices. Clients who are looking for more detailed nutritional programming, such as specific meal plans, recipes, or recommendations for nutritional supplements, should be referred to a registered dietitian.
ACE Personal Trainer Manual, 5th Edition, p. 8–9

7. C. The personal trainer becomes a licensed massage therapist

A personal trainer can provide education about the benefits of massage, but cannot perform hands-on massage therapy for the client, as this would constitute the practice of massage without a license. A personal trainer can teach the client self-myofascial release techniques, such as using a foam roller.
ACE Personal Trainer Manual, 5th Edition, p. 16–17

8. B. They are all accredited by the National Commission for Certifying Agencies.

The NCCA has reviewed and accredited the certification programs for most professions within allied healthcare, including the credentials for registered dietitians, occupational therapists, athletic trainers, podiatrists, nurses, nurse practitioners, massage therapists, personal trainers, group fitness instructors, and advanced fitness professionals.
ACE Personal Trainer Manual, 5th Edition, p. 18

9. B. Unless the personal trainer has other credentials such as an R.D. or M.D., he or she does not possess the qualifications to legally recommend supplements

Personal Trainers can show clients how to utilize the tools available at www.ChooseMyPlate.gov or educating them about the recommendations in the *Dietary Guidelines* to help them gain a better understanding of healthful foods and make better choices. Clients who are looking for more detailed

nutritional programming, such as specific meal plans, recipes, or recommendations for nutritional supplements, should be referred to a registered dietitian.
ACE Personal Trainer Manual, 5th Edition, p. 8–9

10. D. An advanced fitness certification that is NCCA-accredited

By gaining advanced knowledge and skills in a specialized area, a personal trainer can enhance the training services provided to clients. Areas of specialization should be selected by the personal trainer based on his or her desired career path, interests, and client base. The area of specialization should also fall within the scope of practice, or provide the

trainer with knowledge that is complementary to what he or she does within the scope of practice.
ACE Personal Trainer Manual, 5th Edition, p. 21

11. B. 3 to 4 months

There is no single course of study for individuals looking to enter the profession of personal training. Each candidate must select his or her own path based on time, financial resources, learning styles, and personal factors. As a general rule, ACE recommends that candidates allow approximately three to four months of study time on average to adequately prepare for the ACE Personal Trainer Certification Exam.
ACE Personal Trainer Manual, 5th Edition, p. 11

PRINCIPLES OF MOTIVATION
AND ADHERENCE

📖 READING ASSIGNMENT

You should now have completed the reading of Chapter 2 of the *ACE Personal Trainer Manual*, 5th Edition. Carefully review the Summary Review below, as this content highlights valuable information that is particularly relevant to fitness professionals, both in importance and frequency of application or occurrence in the practice of personal training.

Then, answer the Chapter 2 Review Questions and check your answers using the corresponding Answer Key. Review the section in the *ACE Personal Trainer Manual*, 5th Edition, associated with any questions you may have missed.

SUMMARY REVIEW

Fitness professionals have a significant challenge in getting people motivated to start—and then stick with—an exercise program. Personal trainers must learn to maximize the experiences of their clients by enhancing motivation, which leads to increased exercise adherence.

UNDERSTANDING MOTIVATION

Two commonly discussed approaches for evaluating motivation are intrinsic and extrinsic motivation and self-efficacy.

Intrinsic and Extrinsic Motivation

Most clients fall somewhere on the continuum between being intrinsically and extrinsically motivated. Personal trainers should strive to increase a client's situational motivation and empower the client with the perception of control of his or her own participation.

Self-efficacy

By being aware of self-efficacy levels, personal trainers can consistently motivate clients and help them create positive self-belief.

STRATEGIES TO MAINTAIN CLIENT MOTIVATION

Personal trainers can enact strategies to maintain client motivation by effectively educating clients about:

- Social support
- Assertiveness
- Self-regulation
- High-risk situations

FACTORS INFLUENCING EXERCISE PARTICIPATION AND ADHERENCE

The potential determinants for physical activity can be broken down into three categories:

- Personal attributes
  - ✓ Demographic variables
  - ✓ Health status
  - ✓ Activity history
  - ✓ Psychological traits
  - ✓ Knowledge, attitudes, and beliefs
- Environmental factors
  - ✓ Access to facilities
  - ✓ Time
  - ✓ Social support
- Physical-activity factors
  - ✓ Intensity
  - ✓ Injury

FEEDBACK

Types of feedback include:

- Intrinsic
- Extrinsic

LEADERSHIP QUALITIES

The components of being an effective leader include:

- Professionalism
- Client–trainer trust
- The ability to listen effectively
- Excitement for the profession
- Genuine concern for the client

THE PERSONAL TRAINER'S ROLE IN BUILDING ADHERENCE

A personal trainer must be able to effectively build adherence by understanding his or her role in the following areas:

- Program design
- Role clarity
- Goal setting
- Contracts/agreements

GETTING STARTED

This chapter describes the factors that influence exercise adherence and methods for keeping clients involved in their exercise programs. After completing this chapter, you will have a better understanding of:

- The difference between intrinsic and extrinsic motivation
- Strategies to help clients maintain their motivation
- The factors influencing exercise adherence
- Leadership qualities that affect exercise adherence
- The personal trainer's role in building adherence
- The importance of role clarity in establishing the client–trainer relationship
- Properly worded and structured goals

REVIEW QUESTIONS

1. What is the **MOST** important factor for an individual who is starting an exercise program?
   A. Strong support from family and friends
   B. Convenience of the exercise facility
   C. Readiness to change behavior related to exercise
   D. Connecting with a personal trainer

2. Which personal attribute is the **MOST** reliable predictor of an individual's participation in an exercise program?
   A. Weight
   B. Past exercise program participation
   C. Age
   D. Perceived time barriers

3. What is the **MOST** common excuse used by people when dropping out of an exercise program?
   A. Limited access to the exercise facility
   B. A lack of support
   C. Being too old to participate in exercise
   D. A lack of time

4. Which of the following strategies is **BEST** for personal trainers to implement to enhance the likelihood that a client will continue working with them?
   A. Designing the program so the client can work out without having to think much about the exercises
   B. Motivating the client through extrinsic motivators to enhance self-efficacy
   C. Encouraging client ownership of the program to facilitate development of intrinsic motivation
   D. Creating an exercise coaching style based primarily on direction rather than education

5. A person who is confident that he or she can successfully participate regularly in an exercise program **MOST** likely _____.
   A. Has high self-efficacy related to exercise
   B. Is in the contemplation stage of behavioral change
   C. Has very strong self-esteem
   D. Is completely intrinsically motivated

6. Which of the following goals is **MOST** likely to enhance program participation and attainment?
   A. Setting a series of progressively attainable short-term goals
   B. Helping clients keep a primary goal of never missing a session
   C. Setting many goals to ensure some type of program success
   D. Setting only long-term goals to develop adherence

7. A strong social support network can provide an individual with all of the following **EXCEPT** _____.
   A. Improved program adherence
   B. Extrinsic motivation
   C. Relapse-prevention support
   D. Intrinsic motivation

8. Which type of exercise program has a dropout rate almost twice the rate of a moderate-intensity program?
   A. Small-group personal training
   B. Vigorous-intensity exercise program
   C. Home-based personal training
   D. Low-intensity exercise program

9. Which of the following factors is **MOST** likely unrelated to adherence levels in supervised exercise settings?
   A. Education
   B. Age
   C. Income
   D. Gender

10. After one year of regular personal-training sessions, your client wanted to try to continue on her own. During the following six months, you notice your client routinely exercising for one hour, four to five days of the week. Your client says she "loves coming to the gym and feels great after her workouts." You can **MOST** likely contribute your client's success to which of the following?
    A. Extrinsic motivation
    B. Self-esteem
    C. Intrinsic motivation
    D. Self-sufficiency

ANSWER KEY

1. C. Readiness to change behavior related to exercise

The motivation to start a new program can come from any source, but the most important factor in starting an exercise program is the individual. A person cannot be coerced into starting to work out, as he or she must be somewhat ready to make a change.
ACE Personal Trainer Manual, 5th Edition, p. 27

2. B. Past exercise program participation

Activity history is arguably the most important and influential personal attribute variable. In supervised exercise programs, past program participation is the most reliable predictor of current participation. This relationship between past participation and current participation is consistent across gender, obesity, and coronary heart disease status.
ACE Personal Trainer Manual, 5th Edition, p. 34

3. D. A lack of time

A lack of time is the most common excuse for not exercising and for dropping out of an exercise program, as people perceive that they simply do not have time to be physically active. The perception of not having enough time to exercise is likely a reflection of not being interested in or enjoying the activity, or not being committed to the activity program.
ACE Personal Trainer Manual, 5th Edition, p. 35

4. C. Encouraging client ownership of the program to facilitate development of intrinsic motivation

A personal trainer is tasked with fostering how the client generally views exercise and physical activity. The most important thing a personal trainer can do to help build this type of motivation is to empower the client with the perception of control of his or her own participation and to actually give the client control. By encouraging client ownership and involvement in the program and by teaching self-sufficiency and autonomy, personal trainers can help facilitate the development of intrinsic motivation.
ACE Personal Trainer Manual, 5th Edition, p. 29

5. A. Has high self-efficacy related to exercise

In the exercise context, self-efficacy is defined as the belief in one's own capabilities to successfully engage in a physical-activity program. Self-efficacy is positively related to motivation, because when people believe that they can effectively engage in exercise behavior, they do so with a positive attitude and more effort and persistence.
ACE Personal Trainer Manual, 5th Edition, p. 29–30

6. A. Setting a series of progressively attainable short-term goals

Personal trainers should teach their clients the importance of setting SMART goals. The ability of clients to achieve short-term successes in each workout, along with setting a manageable number of attainable long- and short-term goals, will enhance program participation. In contrast, setting only long-term goals gives a client no short-term achievements, setting too many goals can make a client become overwhelmed, and setting negative goals may cause the client to focus on behavior that is to be avoided.
ACE Personal Trainer Manual, 5th Edition, p. 38

7. D. Intrinsic motivation

To be intrinsically motivated, in the exercise context, means that a person is engaged in exercise activity for the inherent pleasure and experience that comes from the engagement itself. Social support is a very important strategy that increases the likelihood of the other listed factors happening.
ACE Personal Trainer Manual, 5th Edition, p. 29 & 31

8. B. Vigorous-intensity exercise program

The drop-out rate in vigorous-intensity exercise programs is almost twice as high as in moderate-intensity activity programs. Additionally, when people are able to choose the type of activity they engage in, six times as many women and more than twice as many men choose to start moderate-intensity programs than vigorous-intensity programs.
ACE Personal Trainer Manual, 5th Edition, p. 35

9. B. Age

Adherence to physical-activity programs has proven to be consistently related to education, income, age, and gender. Specifically, lower levels of activity are seen with increasing age, fewer years of education, and low income. Age, however, has been shown to be unrelated to adherence levels when examined in supervised exercise settings.
ACE Personal Trainer Manual, 5th Edition, p. 34

10. C. Intrinsic motivation

People who are intrinsically motivated report being physically active because they truly enjoy it.
ACE Personal Trainer Manual, 5th Edition, p. 29

COMMUNICATION AND TEACHING TECHNIQUES

You should now have completed the reading of Chapter 3 of the *ACE Personal Trainer Manual*, 5th Edition. Carefully review the Summary Review below, as this content highlights valuable information that is particularly relevant to fitness professionals, both in importance and frequency of application or occurrence in the practice of personal training.

Then, answer the Chapter 3 Review Questions and check your answers using the corresponding Answer Key. Review the section in the *ACE Personal Trainer Manual*, 5th Edition, associated with any questions you may have missed.

SUMMARY REVIEW

Successful personal trainers consistently demonstrate excellent communication and teaching techniques. Positive and productive working relationships between clients and trainers are based on good communication.

STAGES OF THE CLIENT–TRAINER RELATIONSHIP

The early phase of the client–trainer relationship consists of the following four stages, each requiring somewhat different communication skills on the part of the personal trainer:

- Rapport
  - ✓ Making good first impressions
  - ✓ Utilizing verbal communication
  - ✓ Utilizing nonverbal communication
- Investigation stage
  - ✓ Gathering information
  - ✓ Demonstrating effective listening
  - ✓ Responding to difficult disclosures
- Planning stage
  - ✓ Setting goals
  - ✓ Generating and discussing alternatives
  - ✓ Formulating a plan
  - ✓ Evaluating the exercise program
  - ✓ Using motivational interviewing techniques
- Action stage
  - ✓ Setting up self-monitoring systems
  - ✓ Individualizing teaching techniques
  - ✓ Using the "tell, show, do" approach
  - ✓ Providing feedback
  - ✓ Using effective modeling
  - ✓ Creating behavior contracts

STRATEGIES FOR EFFECTIVE COMMUNICATION

Effective communication grows out of personal trainers' knowledge and understanding of, and attitudes toward, their clients.

Cultural Competence Increases Empathy and Rapport

Personal trainers who work with people from different backgrounds can develop cultural competence by taking time to learn about clients' beliefs, attitudes, and lifestyles.

Difficult Clients May Require More Effort

Building rapport with difficult clients may involve more time spent doing the following activities:

- Behaving professionally
- Asking probing questions
- Taking time to understand clients

Empathy and Rapport Enhance Adherence

The time spent establishing a good working relationship enhances adherence to behavior-change programs.

Professional Boundaries Enhance the Effectiveness of Personal Trainers

The professional effectiveness of personal trainers is undermined when they become too personally involved with their clients.

STAGES OF LEARNING AND THEIR APPLICATION TO THE CLIENT–TRAINER RELATIONSHIP

A common model of motor learning divides the process into the following three stages:

- Cognitive stage
- Associative stage
- Autonomous stage

GETTING STARTED

This chapter describes the various stages of the client–trainer relationship, as well as methods of establishing and maintaining a relationship with clients that will enable them to successfully undergo positive lifestyle changes. After completing this chapter, you will have a better understanding of:

- The stages of the client–trainer relationship: rapport, investigation, planning, and action
- Strategies for effective communication
- How cultural competence increases both empathy and rapport, and how they, in turn, enhance adherence
- The stages of learning and their application to the client–trainer relationship
- How to incorporate effective communication and teaching techniques into daily interactions with clients

REVIEW QUESTIONS

1. Which of the following behaviors would **MOST** likely help a trainer develop rapport with a client during the initial session?
   A. Looking away from the client frequently to prevent staring; sitting with good posture and a slight forward lean
   B. Speaking in a soft, friendly voice; leaning against the chair armrest with forearms loosely crossed
   C. Direct, friendly eye contact; maintaining a constant smile and enthusiasm throughout the session
   D. Speaking with confidence; using fluid hand gestures while speaking and quiet hands when listening

2. During the investigation stage, which of the following statements **BEST** pertains to effective listening?
   A. Asking the client closed-ended questions to encourage him or her to share relevant information
   B. Listening carefully to the client while reconstructing the information based on the listener's own beliefs
   C. Asking the client questions and responding to answers with encouraging words and further open-ended questions
   D. Recording detailed notes while the client is speaking

3. A client you have been working with for several months tells you that a close relative recently became seriously ill. Which of the following responses is **MOST** appropriate?
   A. "I'm so sorry. I can't imagine how difficult that must be for you."
   B "Have you considered counseling? Some of my clients have had great success with it."
   C. "I'm sorry! What happened?"
   D "That is terrible! Tell me more about what is worrying you."

4. Which of the following statements **BEST** demonstrates a SMART goal?
   A. "I will improve my cholesterol and blood pressure through better eating and exercise."
   B. "I will run 4 days per week, progressing my run time from 10 to 40 minutes for a 5K in four months."
   C. "I will lose 20 lb (9 kg) for my trip to Hawaii in 2 months by exercising seven days a week."
   D. "I will try a new group exercise class each week to avoid boredom."

5. Which of the following is **MOST** effective in helping a client develop program adherence?
   A. Providing the client with frequent changes in the program to prevent boredom
   B. Having the client self-monitor by keeping an exercise journal
   C. Implementing a reward system for each training session
   D. Conducting fitness assessments every week to measure progresss

6. What is the **MOST** effective way to teach a new exercise to a client?
   A. Show the client how to do the exercise, then have the client perform the exercise while mirroring to provide an example of good form
   B. Tell the client what the exercise is, demonstrate the exercise, and have the client perform the exercise while providing feedback
   C. Use photos of the exercise while explaining it to the client, and then have the client perform the exercise while providing feedback
   D. Have the client perform the exercise while providing verbal instructions to coach him or her through it with proper form

7. A client who is beginning to perform basic body-weight squats with fairly decent form is now ready for more specific feedback to help refine her squatting technique. Which of the following stages of learning is **BEST** represented in this scenario?
    A. Associative
    B. Cognitive
    C. Autonomous
    D. Independent

8. During the initial client investigation stage, which of the following questions is **LEAST** important to ask?
    A. "Can you describe your previous experiences with physical activity?"
    B. "What forms of activity do you like and dislike?"
    C. "Why did you stop exercising in the past?"
    D. "What kind of learner are you—visual, kinesthetic, or auditory?"

9. A client mentions that he prefers tactile feedback and spotting while exercising. This strategy is **MOST** likely indicative of which learning style?
    A. Visual
    B. Associative
    C. Kinesthetic
    D. Cognitive

10. Which of the following strategies is **NOT** a recommended method for practicing motivational interviewing with a client?
    A. Ask probing questions.
    B. Build dependence between trainer and client.
    C. Keep the conversation friendly.
    D. Encourage clients to generate ideas.

ANSWER KEY

1. D. Speaking with confidence; using fluid hand gestures while speaking and quiet hands when listening

Speaking in a voice that is firm and confident will communicate professionalism and direct and friendly eye contact will demonstrate that the client is the center of attention. People tend to be most comfortable when a speaker uses relaxed fluid hand gestures when speaking and quiet hands when listening.
ACE Personal Trainer Manual, 5th Edition, p. 46

2. C. Asking the client questions and responding to answers with encouraging words and further open-ended questions

Effective listening occurs when the personal trainer listens to a client carefully, with empathy, and with an open mind, trying to put him- or herself in the client's shoes. When trying to listen effectively, personal trainers should give clients their full attention.
ACE Personal Trainer Manual, 5th Edition, p. 48–49

3. A. "I'm so sorry. I can't imagine how difficult that must be for you."

Personal trainers are sometimes unsure of how to respond when clients share information that is very sad, such as a disclosure of a client's serious illness, or the illness or death of someone close to the client. Often, a short response is all that is required, such as "I'm so sorry," "That must have been very hard," or "I can't even imagine how difficult that must have been for you and your family." The personal trainer should follow the client's lead as to whether he or she wants to say anything more on a topic.
ACE Personal Trainer Manual, 5th Edition, p. 49

4. B. "I will run 4 days per week, progressing my run time from 10 to 40 minutes for a 5K in four months."

SMART goals should be specific, measurable, attainable, relevant, and time-bound. Goals must contain an estimated timeline as well as be realistically attainable.
ACE Personal Trainer Manual, 5th Edition, p. 50

5. B. Having the client self-monitor by keeping an exercise journal

Research has shown that self-monitoring is one of the most effective ways to support behavioral change, including exercise program adherence and weight loss. Self-monitoring increases client self-awareness by acting as a mirror to give clients a more objective view of their behaviors. Self-monitoring systems also enhance client–trainer communication.
ACE Personal Trainer Manual, 5th Edition, p. 54–55

6. B. Tell the client what the exercise is, demonstrate the exercise, and have the client perform the exercise while providing feedback.

"Tell, show, do" illustrates a good way to introduce a new skill. The personal trainer should begin with a very short explanation of what he or she is going to do and why. The personal trainer should demonstrate the skill accurately and allow clients time to watch. Once the personal trainer has "told and shown," the client is ready to "do," or perform the motor skill. People learn more quickly when they focus on performing the motor skill without being distracted by talking or listening. The personal trainer should observe the client's practice and prepare to give helpful feedback.
ACE Personal Trainer Manual, 5th Edition, p. 56–57

7. A. Associative

In the associative stage of learning, clients begin to master the basics and are ready for more specific feedback that will help them refine the motor skill. So that clients do not learn the skill incorrectly, personal trainers must balance the giving of appropriate feedback with the suitable amount of feedback.
ACE Personal Trainer Manual, 5th Edition, p. 62

8. D. "What kind of learner are you—visual, kinesthetic, or auditory?"

Personal trainers should use the investigation stage not only to learn about a client's current health and fitness, but also to understand a client's exercise likes and dislikes. Personal trainers should ask clients about their previous experiences with physical activity to uncover factors that furthered or disrupted exercise adherence. It is during the action stage that a personal trainer can identify which learning pathway a client prefers by observing actions during learning situations and by listening for clues in language. Once the personal trainer has been working with a particular client for a period of time, his or her preferred learning style should become apparent.
ACE Personal Trainer Manual, 5th Edition, p. 47 & 55

9. C. Kinesthetic

A kinesthetic learner may prefer to be supervised with a hands-on approach and may speak about "feeling" movements, as opposed to a learner who is more auditory or visual in nature.
ACE Personal Trainer Manual, 5th Edition, p. 55

10. B. Build dependence between trainer and client.

Personal trainers should work to build self-confidence in their clients and help clients identify areas of success, no matter how small.
ACE Personal Trainer Manual, 5th Edition, p. 54–55

BASICS OF BEHAVIORAL CHANGE
AND HEALTH PSYCHOLOGY

READING ASSIGNMENT

You should now have completed the reading of Chapter 4 of the *ACE Personal Trainer Manual*, 5th Edition. Carefully review the Summary Review below, as this content highlights valuable information that is particularly relevant to fitness professionals, both in importance and frequency of application or occurrence in the practice of personal training.

Then, answer the Chapter 4 Review Questions and check your answers using the corresponding Answer Key. Review the section in the *ACE Personal Trainer Manual*, 5th Edition, associated with any questions you may have missed.

SUMMARY REVIEW

It is critical that personal trainers understand the psychological and social components of behavior-change practices to help each client adopt and maintain an active lifestyle.

BEHAVIORAL THEORY MODELS

Over the years, numerous explanations have been developed regarding the factors affecting health behaviors. Each of the following models has relevance for personal trainers.

Health Belief Model
- Perceived seriousness of the health problem
- Perceived susceptibility to the health problem
- Cues to action

Self-efficacy
- Past performance experience
- Vicarious experience
- Verbal persuasion
- Physiological state appraisals
- Emotional state and mood appraisals
- Imaginal experiences

Transtheoretical Model of Behavioral Change
- Stages of change
  - ✓ Precontemplation
  - ✓ Contemplation
  - ✓ Preparation
  - ✓ Action
  - ✓ Maintenance
- Important concepts relating to the transtheoretical model of behavioral change
  - ✓ Processes of change
  - ✓ Self-efficacy
  - ✓ Decisional balance
  - ✓ Relapse

Operant Conditioning
- Antecedents
- Consequences

Shaping
- Reinforcing suitable tasks at an appropriate skill level

OBSERVATIONAL LEARNING

All people are influenced to some degree by the behaviors of people around them at home, at work, and in social environments. Trainers should encourage interactions with other people who are also physically active.

COGNITIONS AND BEHAVIOR

Personal trainers should understand what their clients think about exercise and physical activity and lapses in program participation.

BEHAVIOR-CHANGE STRATEGIES

Personal trainers can use the following behavior-change strategies as tools to enhance the likelihood that clients will successfully adopt and maintain a physical-activity program:
- Stimulus control
- Written agreements and behavioral contracting
- Cognitive behavioral techniques
  - ✓ Goal setting
  - ✓ Feedback
  - ✓ Decision making
  - ✓ Self-monitoring

IMPLEMENTING BASIC BEHAVIOR-CHANGE AND HEALTH-PSYCHOLOGY STRATEGIES

Successful personal trainers are able to use communication to gain a better understanding about each client. All information that is gathered through effective communication and observation should be used in program design and implementation.

GETTING STARTED

This chapter addresses the analysis of health behaviors and theories of behavioral change, with special attention given to those related to physical activity and exercise. After completing this chapter, you will have a better understanding of:
- Behavioral theory models, including the health belief model, self-efficacy, and the transtheoretical model of behavioral change
- Principles of behavior change, including operant conditioning and shaping
- How stimulus control can influence behavioral change
- The proper and effective use of written agreements and behavioral contract

REVIEW QUESTIONS

1. During the initial interview with a new client, a trainer learns the client's desire to exercise regularly was based on the results of a recent medical exam revealing prehypertension (blood pressure = 137/88 mmHg), dyslipidemia (total serum cholesterol = 227 mg/dL), and a family history of cardiovascular disease. Based on this information, the client's motivation to exercise is **MOST** likely associated with which of the following components of behavioral change?
   A. Decisional balance

   B. Perceived seriousness

   C. Operant conditioning

   D. Stimulus control

2. On a plane, the gentleman sitting next to you asks a number of questions about exercise, nutrition, and health. He says that he does not currently exercise, but he has been thinking about joining a gym and asks you for recommendations. Based on this information, this gentleman is **MOST** likely in which of the following stages of behavioral change?
   A. Precontemplation

   B. Contemplation

   C. Preparation

   D. Action

3. What is the **MOST** influential source of self-efficacy information related to exercise?
   A. Persuasive verbal feedback

   B. Emotional state and mood

   C. Past exercise performance

   D. Vicarious exercise experiences

4. A new client tells you that she used to participate in local 10K and half-marathon running events before having twins. Although she had wanted to continue running, she has not been active since her children were born two years ago. Now that they are in daycare three days per week, she has begun walking a bit and wants to begin running, with an eventual goal of completing her first marathon. Based on this information, your client has **MOST** likely progressed through which of the following stages of behavioral change from pre-pregnancy to meeting with you today?
   A. Action, precontemplation, action

   B. Maintenance, contemplation, action

   C. Action, maintenance, preparation

   D. Maintenance, contemplation, preparation

5. Which of the following strategies is the **MOST** effective cognitive behavioral technique that a personal trainer can implement to improve client exercise adherence?
   A. Revisiting client goals only during reassessments so they reflect greater progress

   B. Making primary decisions regarding each client's program so that he or she can focus on the exercises

   C. Helping clients move from primarily external feedback to primarily internal feedback

   D. Recording progress so clients can focus on the exercises without having to monitor their own progress

6. According to the principle of operant conditioning, which of the following consequences would be **BEST** for a personal trainer to use to ensure that a desired client behavior will reoccur in the future?
   A. Punishment

   B. Positive reinforcement

   C. Extinction of a positive stimulus

   D. Negative reinforcement

7. Which of the following processes is the **BEST** example of using reinforcement to help a client progress from a quarter lunge to performing a full lunge and then eventually adding resistance?

    A. Shaping

    B. Operant conditioning

    C. Antecedents

    D. Observational learning

8. Which of the following processes is **BEST** exemplified by a client choosing a gym that is in the direct route between home and work?

    A. Operant conditioning

    B. Stimulus control

    C. Imaginal experience

    D. Shaping

9. Which of the following self-monitoring strategies is **MOST** effective for improving clients' long-term program adherence?

    A. Journaling thoughts, experiences, and emotions

    B. Video taping their exercises to see where they can improve

    C. Setting a reminder on their calendar to work out

    D. Analyzing the results of a heart-rate monitor after every session

10. Which of the following strategies would be **MOST** likely to enhance a client's willpower?

    A. Making important behavior-change decisions at the end of the day

    B. Setting many large goals to overhaul one's lifestyle

    C. Planning in advance for moments of weak self-control

    D. Starting a behavior-change plan while applying for new jobs and relocating

ANSWER KEY

1. B. Perceived seriousness

Perceived seriousness is part of the health belief model and refers to the feelings one has about the seriousness of contracting an illness or leaving an illness untreated. The more serious the consequences are perceived to be, the more likely the people are to engage in healthy behavior.
ACE Personal Trainer Manual, 5th Edition, p. 68

2. B. Contemplation

People in the contemplation stage are still sedentary. However, they are starting to consider activity as important and have begun to identify the implications of being inactive.
ACE Personal Trainer Manual, 5th Edition, p. 71–72

3. C. Past exercise performance

The most important and powerful predictor of self-efficacy is past performance experience. This means that an individual who has had past success in adopting and maintaining a physical-activity program will have higher self-efficacy regarding his or her ability to be active in the future. It also means that those individuals with no exercise experience will have much lower self-efficacy regarding their abilities to engage in an exercise program.
ACE Personal Trainer Manual, 5th Edition, p. 70 & 73

4. D. Maintenance, contemplation, preparation

The client started in the maintenance stage, where she participated in regular physical activity for longer than six months. After the birth of her children she moved back into the contemplation stage, where she was sedentary but continued to consider activity important. Now that her children are in day care, she is participating in some physical activity, as she is mentally and physically preparing to adopt a regular activity program. Activity during the preparation stage may be a sporadic walk, or even a periodic visit to the gym, but it is inconsistent. People in the preparation stage are ready to adopt and live an active lifestyle.
ACE Personal Trainer Manual, 5th Edition, p. 71–72

5. C. Helping clients move from primarily external feedback to primarily internal feedback

As efficacy and ability build, trainers should taper off the amount of external feedback they provide, encouraging the clients to start providing feedback for themselves. Clients must learn to reinforce their own behaviors by providing internal encouragement, error correction, and even negative consequences.
ACE Personal Trainer Manual, 5th Edition, p. 82

6. B. Positive reinforcement

According to the principle of operant conditioning, behaviors are strengthened when they are reinforced. In the personal-training context, using reinforcements means that positive or healthy behaviors have consequences that are going to increase the likelihood of the behavior happening again.
ACE Personal Trainer Manual, 5th Edition, p. 76–77

7. A. Shaping

Shaping refers to the process of using reinforcements to gradually achieve a target behavior. This process of continually increasing the demands at an appropriate rate, accompanied by positive reinforcement, leads to the execution of the desired behavior and is a powerful behavior-control and teaching technique.
ACE Personal Trainer Manual, 5th Edition, p. 77–78

8. B. Stimulus control

Stimulus control refers to making adjustments to the environment to increase the likelihood of healthy behaviors. Simple and effective stimulus-control strategies may include choosing a gym that is in the direct route between home and work; keeping a gym bag in the car that contains all the required items for a workout; having workout clothes, socks, and shoes laid out for early morning workouts; and writing down workout times as part of a weekly schedule.
ACE Personal Trainer Manual, 5th Edition, p. 76 & 79–80

9. A. Journaling thoughts, experience, and emotions

Self-monitoring helps a client keep track of program participation and progress. Self-monitoring is most effectively done in the form of keeping a journal that records thoughts, experiences, and emotions that are related to program participation. The gathered information is extremely helpful in developing an effective plan for long-term adherence.
ACE Personal Trainer Manual, 5th Edition, p. 82

10. C. Planning in advance for moments of weak self-control

Given that willpower is inherently limited, clients should have strategies to conserve it. Planning in advance for moments of weak self-control reinforces willpower when it is needed most.
ACE Personal Trainer Manual, 5th Edition, p. 80

UNDERSTANDING THE ACE INTEGRATED
FITNESS TRAINING® MODEL

 READING ASSIGNMENT

You should now have completed the reading of Chapter 5 of the *ACE Personal Trainer Manual,* 5th Edition. Carefully review the Summary Review below, as this content highlights valuable information that is particularly relevant to fitness professionals, both in importance and frequency of application or occurrence in the practice of personal training.

Then, answer the Chapter 5 Review Questions and check your answers using the corresponding Answer Key. Review the section in the *ACE Personal Trainer Manual,* 5th Edition, associated with any questions you may have missed.

SUMMARY REVIEW

A personal trainer should be familiar with the following concepts related to providing services as a fitness professional:
- Traditional physiological training parameters versus new physiological training parameters
- General exercise recommendations for healthy adults

FUNCTION–HEALTH–FITNESS–PERFORMANCE CONTINUUM

A personal trainer should understand the function–health–fitness–performance continuum and how it relates to individual client exercise programming.

INTRODUCTION TO THE ACE INTEGRATED FITNESS TRAINING MODEL

ACE Certified Personal Trainers should understand the following terms and concepts related to the ACE Integrated Fitness Training (ACE IFT®) Model and how each influences the development, implementation, and/or progression of a client's exercise program:
- Assessment sequencing for the general client
- ACE IFT Model phases and the function–health–fitness–performance continuum
- Rapport
- Behavioral strategies
- Training components and phases

Because functional movement and resistance training are integral parts of the ACE IFT Model, an ACE Certified Personal Trainer should understand how these modalities are represented in the following content areas:
- Phase 1: Stability and mobility training
  - ✓ Basic assessments
- Phase 2: Movement training
  - ✓ Five primary movements of exercise
- Phase 3: Load training
  - ✓ Periodization
- Phase 4: Performance training
  - ✓ Power, speed, agility, and quickness

Because cardiorespiratory training is an integral part of the ACE IFT Model, an ACE Certified Personal Trainer should understand how this mode of exercise is represented in the following content areas:

- Phase 1: Aerobic-base training
  - ✓ First ventilatory threshold (VT1)
- Phase 2: Aerobic-efficiency training
  - ✓ Second ventilatory threshold (VT2)
- Phase 3: Anaerobic-endurance training
  - ✓ Three-zone intensity model
- Phase 4: Anaerobic-power training

SPECIAL POPULATION CLIENTELE

ACE Certified Personal Trainers working with special-population clients should understand how to utilize the integrated training process provided in the ACE IFT Model, being sure to adjust exercise selection, intensity, sets, repetitions, and duration to fit the special needs of each client.

GETTING STARTED

This chapter introduces the ACE IFT Model. After completing this chapter, you will have a better understanding of:

- The function–health–fitness–performance continuum
- How rapport and behavioral strategies fit within this training model
- The training components and phases of the model, including functional movement and resistance training and cardiorespiratory training

REVIEW QUESTIONS

1. What foundational element is the ACE IFT Model built upon?
   A. Health improvement
   B. Functional fitness
   C. Developing rapport
   D. Cardiorespiratory fitness

2. What assessments are essential according to the ACE IFT Model and should be completed prior to a client beginning an exercise program?
   A. Assessing posture, functional movement, and muscular strength and endurance
   B. Collecting health-history data to identify contraindications for exercise and the need for referral
   C. Assessing cardiorespiratory fitness using the submaximal talk test to determine HR at VT1
   D. Measuring body composition and waist-to-hip ratio

3. Which of the following is **MOST** likely to create a barrier to fitness-related behavioral change for some clients?
   A. Identifying a client's readiness to change behavior
   B. Creating early positive exercise experiences
   C. Implementing strategies for working with clients based on their personality styles
   D. Conducting initial comprehensive assessments of fitness and body composition

4. What are the five primary movements that are the focus of the movement-training phase?
   A. Squatting, lunging, swinging, throwing, and arching movements
   B. Jumping, hopping, pushing, pulling, and arching movements
   C. Squatting, lunging, pushing, pulling, and rotational movements
   D. Jumping, hopping, swinging, throwing, and rotational movements

5. In what phase of the functional movement and resistance training component of the ACE IFT Model would a person be categorized if he has lumbar lordosis, limited range of motion in the hips and shoulders, and performs resistance-training workouts four days per week?
   A. Phase 1: Stability and mobility training
   B. Phase 2: Movement training
   C. Phase 3: Load training
   D. Phase 4: Performance training

6. Strength training, body building, and training for muscular endurance all fall under which functional movement and resistance training phase of the ACE IFT Model?
   A. Phase 1: Stability and mobility training
   B. Phase 2: Movement training
   C. Phase 3: Load training
   D. Phase 4: Performance training

7. Performance training includes speed, agility, quickness, and reactivity drills that would be **MOST** appropriate for which of the following clients?
   A. 45-year-old male competitive tennis player
   B. 33-year-old female marathon runner
   C. 27-year-old male body builder
   D. 52-year-old female recreational golfer

8. A regular group exercise participant with no competitive goals would be classified in which phase of the cardiorespiratory training component of the ACE IFT Model?
   A. Phase 1: Aerobic-base training
   B. Phase 2: Aerobic-efficiency training
   C. Phase 3: Anaerobic-endurance training
   D. Phase 4: Anaerobic-power training

9. Personal trainers can use the talk test as an
    upper limit for exercise intensity to determine if a
    client is exercising below which of the following
    cardiorespiratory markers?

    A. $\dot{V}O_2$max

    B. Second ventilatory threshold (VT2)

    C. Anaerobic threshold

    D. First ventilatory threshold (VT1)

10. Cardiorespiratory exercise in zone 2 is performed at
    what intensity?

    A. Below VT1

    B. At VT1

    C. From VT1 to just below VT2

    D. At or above VT2

ANSWER KEY

1. C. Developing rapport

The foundation of the ACE IFT Model is built upon rapport. Successful personal trainers consistently demonstrate excellent communication skills and teaching techniques, while understanding the psychological, emotional, and physiological needs and concerns of their clients. Building rapport is a critical component of successful client–trainer relationships, as this process promotes open communication, develops trust, and fosters the client's desire to participate in an exercise program.
ACE Personal Trainer Manual, 5th Edition, p. 93

2. B. Collecting health-history data to identify contraindications for exercise and the need for referral

After establishing initial rapport, the trainer should collect health-history information to determine if the client has any contraindications or requires a physician's evaluation prior to exercise. This process helps ensure the safety of the client and provide an opportunity for the personal trainer to establish trust and create an open source of communication.
ACE Personal Trainer Manual, 5th Edition, p. 93–94

3. D. Conducting initial comprehensive assessments of fitness and body composition

Exercise programming has traditionally had a primary focus on helping clients make physiological changes, placing early emphasis on fitness assessments for program design and tracking progress. However, to the out-of-shape client, a complete battery of initial assessments can be detrimental to early program success by reinforcing his or her negative self-image and beliefs that he or she is hopelessly out of shape or overweight.
ACE Personal Trainer Manual, 5th Edition, p. 95–96

4. C. Squatting, lunging, pushing, pulling, and rotational movements

Bend-and-lift movements (e.g., squatting); single-leg movements (e.g., lunging); pushing movements (e.g., during a push-up exercise or when pushing open a door); pulling movements (e.g., bent-over row, pull-up, opening a car door, or picking up a child); and rotational (spiral) movements are the five basic movement patterns that make up the foundation of the movement-training phase.
ACE Personal Trainer Manual, 5th Edition, p. 99

5. A. Phase 1: Stability and mobility training

The training focus during phase 1 is on the introduction of low-intensity exercise programs to improve muscle balance, muscular endurance, core function, flexibility, and static and dynamic balance to improve the client's posture. Exercise selection in phase 1 focuses on core and balance exercises that improve the strength and function of the tonic muscles responsible for stabilizing the spine and center of gravity during movement. This client has postural issues that need to be addressed with stability and mobility exercises before continuing resistance-training workouts.
ACE Personal Trainer Manual, 5th Edition, p. 98

6. C. Phase 3: Load training

In phase 3, load training, the exercise program is advanced with the addition of an external force or increasing the external load, placing emphasis on muscle force production where the variables of training can be manipulated to address a variety of exercise goals. These goals may include positive changes in body composition, muscular strength, muscle hypertrophy, or muscular endurance, or simply looking more "toned."
ACE Personal Trainer Manual, 5th Edition, p. 100

7. A. 45-year-old male competitive tennis player

Phase 4 of the functional movement and resistance-training component emphasizes specific training to improve speed, agility, quickness, reactivity, and power. This type of training is appropriate for clients who have athletic or performance-oriented goals.
ACE Personal Trainer Manual, 5th Edition, p. 101

8. B. Phase 2: Aerobic-efficiency training

Phase 2, aerobic-efficiency training, is dedicated to enhancing the client's aerobic efficiency by progressing the program through increased duration of sessions, increased frequency of sessions when possible, and the introduction of aerobic intervals. These training characteristics are common in typical group fitness programs. Because there are aerobic intervals included in this phase, the training stimulus will be adequate for some clients to perform cardiorespiratory exercise in phase 2 for many years if they have no goals of improving speed or fitness beyond that gained in phase 2 training.
ACE Personal Trainer Manual, 5th Edition, p. 103–104

9. D. First ventilatory threshold (VT1)

To enhance exercise program design, trainers can conduct the submaximal talk test to determine heart rate at VT1. The talk test can also be used to help clients gain a better understanding of RPE, as VT1 has been found to be approximately between an RPE of 4 and 5 ("somewhat strong" to "strong").
ACE Personal Trainer Manual, 5th Edition, p. 104

10. C. From VT1 to just below VT2

Aerobic intervals at or just above VT1 and below VT2 [Rating of perceived exertion (RPE) of 5] during one or two cardiorespiratory sessions per week promote aerobic efficiency in zone 2.
ACE Personal Trainer Manual, 5th Edition, p. 106

6

BUILDING RAPPORT AND THE INITIAL INVESTIGATION STAGE

READING ASSIGNMENT

You should now have completed the reading of Chapter 6 of the *ACE Personal Trainer Manual,* 5th Edition. Carefully review the Summary Review below, as this content highlights valuable information that is particularly relevant to fitness professionals, both in importance and frequency of application or occurrence in the practice of personal training.

Then, answer the Chapter 6 Review Questions and check your answers using the corresponding Answer Key. Review the section in the *ACE Personal Trainer Manual,* 5th Edition, associated with any questions you may have missed.

SUMMARY REVIEW

It is imperative for a personal trainer to make a strong and positive first impression. The following three attributes are essential for successful relationships:

- Empathy
- Warmth
- Genuineness

There are four essential stages in building client–trainer relationships:

- Rapport
- Investigation
- Planning
- Action

A personal trainer must be aware of the following factors that can affect communication between the client and fitness professional:

- Environment
- Empathy
- Effective communication
- Interviewing techniques

FACILITATING CHANGE AND MOTIVATIONAL INTERVIEWING

A personal trainer should understand theoretical models of behavioral change, such as the transtheoretical model of behavioral change, and have knowledge of motivational interviewing techniques for enhancing a client's intrinsic motivation to change.

THE HEALTH-RISK APPRAISAL

A personal trainer must have a thorough understanding of the following concepts related to health-risk appraisal:

- The purposes of the pre-participation screen
- Whether the exercise program is self-directed or being conducted under the consultation and supervision of a qualified fitness professional
- The basis for, and importance of, performing a risk stratification prior to engaging in a physical-activity program
- The three basic steps for performing a risk stratification
- The signs and symptoms of coronary artery disease (CAD)
- Atherosclerotic cardiovascular disease risk factor thresholds for use with American College of Sports Medicine (ACSM) risk stratification

EVALUATION FORMS

A personal trainer should have an understanding of common evaluation forms for use with clients:

- Physical Activity Readiness Questionnaire (PAR-Q)
- CAD health-risk assessment
- Informed consent
- Agreement and release of liability
- Health-history questionnaire
- Exercise history and attitude questionnaire

HEALTH CONDITIONS THAT AFFECT PHYSICAL ACTIVITY

Personal trainers should have an understanding of how the following health conditions and medications affect physical activity:

- Cardiovascular disease
- Respiratory problems
- Metabolic disorders
- Pregnancy
- Antihypertensive medication
- Cold medications
- Hypertension
- Musculoskeletal problems
- Hernia
- Illness or infection
- Bronchodilators

SEQUENCING ASSESSMENTS

The following concepts are related to the selection, timing, and sequencing of client assessments:

- The appropriateness of conducting assessments with clients
- Physiological influences on assessment
- Signs and symptoms that merit immediate test termination and referral to a more qualified healthcare professional
- Professionalism and the testing environment

CHOOSING THE RIGHT ASSESSMENTS

A personal trainer should take into account the following factors when choosing health/fitness assessments for their clients:

- Goals of the assessment
- Testing environment
- Age of the participant
- Physical limitations of the participant
- Availability of equipment

CONDUCTING ESSENTIAL CARDIOVASCULAR ASSESSMENTS

Personal trainers should have an understanding of the following assessments and the impact of the assessment results on a client's program design:

- Heart rate (exercise and resting)
- Blood pressure
- Exercise-induced feeling inventory

RATINGS OF PERCEIVED EXERTION

Knowledge of common trends relating to, and recommendations for use of, subjective scales of ratings of perceived exertion is essential for personal trainers.

GETTING STARTED

This chapter covers the earliest stages of the client–trainer relationship. After completing this chapter, you will have a better understanding of:

- Facilitating change and motivational interviewing
- How to perform a health-risk appraisal and utilize common forms
- How various health conditions and medications affect the body's response to exercise
- How to choose and schedule assessments so that the process is appropriate for each client
- How to accurately measure clients' heart rate and blood pressure

REVIEW QUESTIONS

1. Which of the stages of a successful client–trainer relationship includes implementing strategies to improve motivation and promote long-term adherence?
    A. Rapport
    B. Investigation
    C. Planning
    D. Action

2. What is the name of the essential attribute of successful relationships that is described as "the ability to respect another person regardless of his or her uniqueness?"
    A. Empathy
    B. Warmth
    C. Genuineness
    D. Honesty

3. "Can you tell me more about the circumstances surrounding the times you have experienced low-back soreness?" is an example of what type of interviewing technique?
    A. Reflecting
    B. Confronting
    C. Informing
    D. Probing

4. What is this client's "total score" for atherosclerotic cardiovascular disease using the ACSM risk factor thresholds?
    A. +1
    B. +2
    C. +3
    D. +4

5. According to the ACSM risk stratification, what is this client's level of risk?
    A. Low risk
    B. Moderate risk
    C. High risk
    D. Very high risk

6. What are the recommendations regarding exercise testing based on this client's risk stratification?
    A. Trainer can perform submaximal fitness testing without a physician's supervision
    B. A medical exam is required before moderate exercise
    C. A physician should be present for all submaximal and maximal fitness testing
    D. A graded exercise test is required prior to beginning a moderate exercise program

USE THE FOLLOWING CLIENT INFORMATION TO ANSWER QUESTIONS 4–6:

Gender: Male

Age: 47 years

Family history: Mother has hypertension; father had coronary bypass surgery at age 59

Smoking: Quit smoking 20 years ago

Current exercise: Walks dog 1–2 times per day for 10 minutes per walk

BMI: 29 kg/m^2

Blood pressure: 132/86 mmHg

Total serum cholesterol: 216 mg/dL

LDL cholesterol: 138 mg/dL

HDL cholesterol: 48 mg/dL

Fasting plasma glucose: 94 mg/dL

Goals: Lose 20 lb (9 kg); increase muscle strength and cardiorespiratory fitness

USE THE FOLLOWING CLIENT INFORMATION TO ANSWER QUESTIONS 7–8:

Gender: Female

Age: 39 years

Family history: Father has type 1 diabetes; Mother just diagnosed with type 2 diabetes

Smoking: Never smoked

Current exercise: Swims 3–4 days per week for 30–45 minutes for the past 6 months

BMI: 31 kg/m^2

Blood pressure: 128/82 mmHg

Total serum cholesterol: 224 mg/dL

LDL cholesterol: 122 mg/dL

HDL cholesterol: 64 mg/dL

Fasting plasma glucose: 95 mg/dL

Goals: Lose 30 lb (13.5 kg); enhance exercise program and improve diet to prevent diabetes

7. What is this client's "total score" for atherosclerotic cardiovascular disease using the ACSM risk factor thresholds?

    A. 0

    B. +1

    C. +2

    D. +3

8. What are the recommendations regarding the intensity of the cardiorespiratory exercise program and the need for a medical examination and graded exercise test based on this client's risk stratification?

    A. The trainer can design a program with the client performing moderate-intensity exercise, but a medical exam and exercise test would be recommended prior to vigorous-intensity exercise.

    B. The trainer can design a program with the client performing moderate- or vigorous-intensity exercise without the client needing a medical exam or exercise test.

    C. An exercise test is recommended prior to moderate-intensity exercise, and a medical exam and exercise test are recommended prior to vigorous-intensity exercise.

    D. A medical exam and graded exercise test are required prior to beginning an exercise program.

9. Your new client is a 57-year-old woman who plays golf, tennis, and squash avidly. Her health-risk appraisal reveals only one positive risk factor (age) and that she has a heart murmur. According to the ACSM risk stratification, what is this client's level of risk?

    A. Low risk

    B. Moderate risk

    C. High risk

    D. Very high risk

10. Which evaluation form does a client sign to acknowledge that he or she has been educated about, and understands, the risks associated with being active?

    A. Agreement and release of liability waiver

    B. Medical release

    C. Exercise history and attitude questionnaire

    D. Informed consent

11. A personal trainer could design an exercise program without requiring a physician's release prior to participation for which of the following?

    A. 42-year-old female client who has lumbar lordosis

    B. 54-year-old male client who has type 2 diabetes

    C. 61-year-old female client who takes a calcium channel blocker

    D. 35-year-old male client who has asthma

12. Which of the following responses is a relative contraindication for weightlifting unless cleared by a physician?

    A. Diabetes

    B. Hernia

    C. Pregnancy

    D. Infection

ANSWER KEY

1. D. Action

The action stage involves the successful implementation of all programming components and providing the appropriate instruction, feedback, and progression as needed. This stage includes: instruction, demonstration, and execution of programs; implementing strategies to improve motivation and promote long-term adherence; providing feedback and evaluation; making necessary adjustments to programs; and monitoring the overall exercise experience and progression toward goals.
ACE Personal Trainer Manual, 5th Edition, p. 111

2. B. Warmth

Warmth is an unconditional positive regard, or respect, for another person regardless of his or her individuality and uniqueness. This quality will convey a climate that communicates safety and acceptance to the client.
ACE Personal Trainer Manual, 5th Edition, p. 111

3. D. Probing

Probing is the strategy of asking additional questions in an attempt to gather more information (e.g., "Please tell me more about the medications you are taking").
ACE Personal Trainer Manual, 5th Edition, p. 114

4. C. +3

The following ACSM CAD risk factor thresholds result in the client's score of +3: +1 for Age: (men) ≥45 years; +1 for sedentary lifestyle; +1 for LDL cholesterol: ≥130 mg/dL.
ACE Personal Trainer Manual, 5th Edition, p. 120

5. B. Moderate risk

The stratification between low-, moderate-, and high-risk individuals requires differentiation between one and two risk factors, and the symptoms or medical diagnosis of diseases. Moderate risk is indicated when an individual is asymptomatic with ≥2 total risk factors.
ACE Personal Trainer Manual, 5th Edition, 121

6. A. Trainer can perform submaximal fitness testing without a physician's supervision

A moderate-risk client can perform submaximal fitness testing without the presence of a doctor.
ACE Personal Trainer Manual, 5th Edition, p. 121

7. A. 0

The following ACSM CAD risk factor thresholds result in the client's score of 0: BMI ≥30 kg/m^2 results in +1, whereas HDL cholesterol ≥60 mg/dL results in a –1.
ACE Personal Trainer Manual, 5th Edition, p. 120

8. B. The trainer can design a program with the client performing moderate- or vigorous-intensity exercise without the client needing a medical exam or exercise test.

A low-risk client can perform moderate- to vigorous-intensity exercise without a prior medical exam or exercise test.
ACE Personal Trainer Manual, 5th Edition, p. 121

9. C. High risk

This client has a known sign and symptom of a heart disorder (i.e., heart murmur), which automatically places her in the high-risk category.
ACE Personal Trainer Manual, 5th Edition, p. 121–122

10. D. Informed consent

When a client signs an informed consent form, he or she is acknowledging having been specifically informed about the risks associated with activity.
ACE Personal Trainer Manual, 5th Edition, p. 122–123

11. A. 42-year-old female client who has lumbar lordosis

If a client has no contraindications for exercise, but presents with lumbar lordosis, he or she can begin working with a personal trainer and following a fitness program.
ACE Personal Trainer Manual, 5th Edition, p. 120–121

12. B. Hernia

A hernia is a relative contraindication for weight lifting unless cleared by a physician. If there is a history of a hernia, it is very important for the trainer to instruct and educate the client on proper breathing and lifting techniques.
ACE Personal Trainer Manual, 5th Edition, p. 131

FUNCTIONAL ASSESSMENTS:
POSTURE, MOVEMENT, CORE, BALANCE, AND FLEXIBILITY

📖 READING ASSIGNMENT

You should now have completed the reading of Chapter 7 of the *ACE Personal Trainer Manual,* 5th Edition. Carefully review the Summary Review below, as this content highlights valuable information that is particularly relevant to fitness professionals, both in importance and frequency of application or occurrence in the practice of personal training.

Then, answer the Chapter 7 Review Questions and check your answers using the corresponding Answer Key. Review the section in the *ACE Personal Trainer Manual,* 5th Edition, associated with any questions you may have missed.

SUMMARY REVIEW

One primary objective of all training programs should be to improve functionality to help clients enhance their abilities to perform activities of daily living (ADL). Since posture is the foundation for all movement, personal trainers should incorporate assessments to evaluate static posture. Trainers should also incorporate movement screens to evaluate movement compensations in their clients.

STATIC POSTURAL ASSESSMENT

A static postural assessment may offer valuable insight into:
- Muscle imbalance at a joint and the working relationships of muscles around a joint
- Altered neural action of the muscles moving and controlling the joint

Muscle imbalance and postural deviations can be attributed to many factors that are both correctible and non-correctible, including the following:
- Correctible factors
  - ✓ Repetitive movements
  - ✓ Awkward positions and movements
  - ✓ Side dominance
  - ✓ Lack of joint stability
  - ✓ Lack of joint mobility
  - ✓ Imbalanced strength-training programs
- Non-correctible factors
  - ✓ Congenital conditions
  - ✓ Some pathologies
  - ✓ Structural deviations
  - ✓ Certain types of trauma

Personal trainers should be familiar with the protocols for the assessment of, and the practical implications of, the following five common postural deviations:
- Foot pronation/supination and the effect on tibial and femoral rotation
- Hip adduction
- Hip tilting (anterior or posterior)
- Shoulder position and the thoracic spine
- Head position

MOVEMENT SCREENS

Movement can essentially be broken down and described by five primary movements that people perform during many daily activities:

- Bending/raising and lifting/lowering movements
- Single-leg movements
- Pushing movements and resultant movement
- Pulling movements and resultant movement
- Rotational movements

Personal trainers should be familiar with the protocols for the following common movement screens, as well as the practical implications for clients who have challenges with these screens:

- Bend and lift screen
- Hurdle step screen
- Shoulder push stabilization screen
- Thoracic spine mobility screen

FLEXIBILITY AND MUSCLE-LENGTH TESTING

Personal trainers should be familiar with the protocols for the following common flexibility and muscle-length tests, as well as the practical implications for clients who have challenges with these tests:

- Thomas test for hip flexion/quadriceps length
- Passive straight-leg (PSL) raise
- Shoulder flexion and extension
- Internal and external rotation of the humerus at the shoulder
- Apley's scratch test for shoulder mobility

BALANCE AND THE CORE

Personal trainers should be familiar with the protocols for the following common balance and core function tests, as well as the practical implications for clients who have challenges with these tests:

- Sharpened Romberg test
- Stork-stand balance test
- McGill's torso muscular endurance test battery

GETTING STARTED

This chapter explains the importance of various functional assessments and outlines how to properly perform each. After completing this chapter, you will have a better understanding of:

- How to set up a plumb line for use in postural assessments
- The five key postural deviations
- How to conduct various movement screens, including clearing tests
- How to conduct flexibility and muscle-length testing
- How to test for shoulder mobility, as well as balance and core function

REVIEW QUESTIONS

1. During a static postural assessment, in which plane of movement does the personal trainer view the client's balanced resting posture between the anterior and posterior sides of the body?
   A. Frontal
   B. Sagittal
   C. Coronal
   D. Transverse

2. Which of the following responses correctly describes a phenomenon called "winged scapulae?"
   A. A protrusion of the inferior angle and vertebral (medial) border of the scapula
   B. A protrusion of the vertebral (medial) border outward
   C. A protrusion of the superior angle and spine of the scapula
   D. A protrusion of the inferior angle and glenohumeral (lateral) border of the scapula

3. Which of the following observations would **NOT** be noted as a postural deviation?
   A. The palms of the hands face backward
   B. The superior, anterior portion of the pelvis rotates downward and forward
   C. TThe cheek bone is in line with the collar bone
   D. The subtalar joint is in pronation

4. Which of the following postural deviations could indicate that a client has an internally (medially) rotated humerus and/or scapular protraction?
   A. Front view: palms face backward
   B. Posterior view: scapular winging visible
   C. Side view: upper back has an exaggerated curve
   D. Front view: sternum not in line with plumb line

5. A client should be referred to his or her physician if which of the following is found during assessments?
   A. Lordosis during postural screening
   B. A lack of foot stability with the ankle collapsing inwardt
   C. Pain during the bend and lift screen
   D. Forward-head position during postural screening

6. During the bend and lift screen, which observation could indicate that the client has tight plantarflexors?
   A. Hamstrings touch the calves
   B. Squat initiated at knees
   C. The big toes extend upward
   D. Heels rise off the floor

7. During the hurdle step screen, you observe a client exhibiting an anterior pelvic tilt and a forward torso lean as he steps forward. Which compensation **MOST** likely causes this?
   A. Weak gluteus medius and maximus
   B. Tight stance-leg hip flexors
   C. Weak stance-leg hip adductors
   D. Tight ankle plantarflexors

8. During the Thomas test, you observe that your client can lower her right thigh to about 10 degrees above the table with the knee flexed at about 90 degrees. Based on these observations, which of the following notes would you make?
   A. Right leg has normal range of motion
   B. Tightness in the right rectus femoris
   C. Limited range of motion in lumbar spine
   D. Tightness in the right iliopsoas

9. The passive straight-leg (PSL) raise test assesses the length of which of the following muscle groups?
   A. Iliopsoas
   B. Gluteals
   C. Hamstrings
   D. Quadriceps

10. Which of the following observations during the passive straight-leg (PSL) raise represents normal length of the hamstrings?
    A. Raised leg achieves 70 degrees of movement
    B. Pelvis rotates posteriorly after the raised leg passes 70 degrees of movement
    C. Raised leg stops just short of 90 degrees of movement
    D. Opposite leg lifts off the mat as the raised leg approaches 80 degrees of movement

11. While having a client perform the external and internal rotation test, you observe that he can rotate the forearms internally about 50 degrees toward the mat and externally to about 90 degrees so that the arms touch the mat. Based on these observations, which of the following notes would you make?

    A. Good mobility for both internal and external rotators

    B. Tight internal rotators; good mobility for external rotators

    C. Tight external rotators; good mobility for internal rotators

    D. Tightness in both internal and external rotators

12. What is the purpose of stability and mobility training?

    A. Restorative exercise to improve posture and movement compensations found through functional and postural assessments

    B. Teaching correct squat, lunge, push, pull, and rotational movement patterns

    C. To prepare the body for sports conditioning and performance training

    D. Rehabilitative exercise to restore function following injury or surgery

13. Scapular winging during the shoulder push stabilization screen would **MOST** likely be due to

    _____.

    A. Weak core and low back

    B. Scapulothoracic joint instability

    C. Curved thoracic spine

    D. Strong serratus anterior

ANSWER KEY

1. B. Sagittal

The right-angle model used in static postural assessment implies a state from a frontal view wherein the two hemispheres (left and right) are equally divided, and from a sagittal view wherein the anterior and posterior surfaces appear in balance.
ACE Personal Trainer Manual, 5th Edition, p. 154

2. A. A protrusion of the inferior angle and vertebral (medial) border of the scapula

While looking at the client from the posterior view, if the vertebral (medial) and/or inferior angle of the scapulae protrude outward, this indicates an inability of the scapular stabilizers (primarily the rhomboids and serratus anterior) to hold the scapulae in place. Noticeable protrusion of the vertebral (medial) border outward is termed "scapular protraction," while protrusion of the inferior angle and vertebral (medial) border outward is termed "winged scapulae."
ACE Personal Trainer Manual, 5th Edition, p. 161–162

3. C. The cheek bone is in line with the collar bone

With good posture, the cheek bone and collar bone should almost be in vertical alignment with each other. The palms of the hands facing backward indicates a scapular protraction deviation; the superior, anterior portion of the pelvis rotating downward and forward indicates an anterior tilt of the pelvis deviation; and when the subtalar joint is in pronation, this deviation can cause internal rotation at the knee and hip.
ACE Personal Trainer Manual, 5th Edition, p. 163

4. A. Front view: palms face backward

Scapular protraction can be identified from the anterior view. If the palms face backward when the hands are positioned at the sides, this generally indicates internal (medial) rotation of the humerus and/or scapular protraction.
ACE Personal Trainer Manual, 5th Edition, p. 162

5. C. Pain during the bend and lift screen

If the client experiences pain during a movement screen, the test should be stopped and the client should be referred to his or her healthcare provider to have the painful area evaluated before performing that type of movement in a future exercise session.
ACE Personal Trainer Manual, 5th Edition, p. 167

6. D. Heels rise off the floor

An inability to keep the heels on the floor during the bend and lift screen could be indicative of tight calf musculature (i.e., plantarflexors).
ACE Personal Trainer Manual, 5th Edition, p. 168

7. B. Tight stance-leg hip flexors

An anterior pelvic tilt and forward torso lean during the hurdle step screen could indicate tight stance-leg hip flexors and weak rectus abdominis and back extensors.
ACE Personal Trainer Manual, 5th Edition, p. 172

8. D. Tightness in the right iliopsoas

An inability to lay the back of the right thigh completely flat on the table during the Thomas test could indicate a tightness of the right iliopsoas, which is preventing the hip from rotating posteriorly and inhibiting the thigh from being able to touch the table.
ACE Personal Trainer Manual, 5th Edition, p. 179–180

9. C. Hamstrings

The passive straight-leg (PSL) raise test assesses the length of the hamstrings with the pelvis held in neutral position.
ACE Personal Trainer Manual, 5th edition, p. 180

10. C. Raised leg stops just short of 90 degrees of movement

Normal length of the hamstrings in the passive straight-leg test is indicated when the raised leg achieves ≥80 degrees of movement before the pelvis rotates posteriorly.
ACE Personal Trainer Manual, 5th edition, p. 180–181

11. C. Tight external rotators; good mobility for internal rotators

The inability to internally rotate the forearms to at least 70 degrees of rotation (i.e., this client could only reach 50 degrees) toward the mat indicates tight external rotators. The ability to externally rotate the forearms 90 degrees to touch the mat (i.e., this client can reach the 90 degrees and the arms touch the mat) indicates good mobility in the internal rotators.
ACE Personal Trainer Manual, 5th Edition, p. 183–184

12. A. Restorative exercise to improve posture and movement compensations

Phase 1, stability and mobility exercise, is designed to improve posture and movement compensation, thus restoring good joint alignment and muscle balance.
ACE Personal Trainer Manual, 5th Edition, p. 156

13. B. Scapulothoracic joint instability

Scapular winging during the shoulder push stabilization screen most likely indicates an inability of the parascapular muscles (i.e., serratus anterior, trapezius, levator scapula, and rhomboids) to stabilize the scapulae against the rib cage.
ACE Personal Trainer Manual, 5th Edition, p. 173–174

PHYSIOLOGICAL
ASSESSMENTS

 READING ASSIGNMENT

You should now have completed the reading of Chapter 8 of the *ACE Personal Trainer Manual*, 5th Edition. Carefully review the Summary Review below, as this content highlights valuable information that is particularly relevant to fitness professionals, both in importance and frequency of application or occurrence in the practice of personal training.

Then, answer the Chapter 8 Review Questions and check your answers using the corresponding Answer Key. Review the section in the *ACE Personal Trainer Manual*, 5th Edition, associated with any questions you may have missed.

SUMMARY REVIEW

A personal trainer should have knowledge and practical skills in both health-related assessments and sports- or skill-related assessments that are relevant to a client's program development and ongoing evaluation.

TESTING AND MEASUREMENT

A personal trainer should have knowledge of the potential resources for gaining hands-on training in fitness assessments. Personal trainers must be aware of identifiable signs or symptoms that merit immediate exercise-test termination and referral to a qualified healthcare professional.

ANTHROPOMETRIC MEASUREMENTS AND BODY COMPOSITION

A general understanding of following anthropometric measurements is important for all personal trainers:
- Bioelectrical impedance analysis (BIA)
- Air displacement plethysmography (ADP)
- Dual-energy x-ray absorptiometry (DEXA)
- Hydrostatic weighing
- Near-infrared interactance (NIR)
- Total body electrical conductivity (TOBEC)

A personal trainer should have a general understanding of the appropriate use of, protocol for, and programming considerations related to the following anthropometric measurements:
- Skinfold measurement
- Body mass index (BMI)
- Girth measurements
- Waist-to-hip ratio
- Waist circumference

CARDIORESPIRATORY FITNESS TESTING

For the safe and effective administration of physical-fitness tests, a personal trainer should have knowledge of the following concepts related to cardiorespiratory fitness (CRF) testing:

- Appropriate use of, and reasons for, administering CRF tests
- $\dot{V}O_2$max assessments versus submaximal CRF tests
- Variables related to the lack of accuracy in estimated maximal oxygen uptake assessments
- Methods available for determining maximal heart rate (MHR)
- Cardiorespiratory assessments for the lab or fitness center

A personal trainer should have a general understanding of the appropriate use of, protocol for, and programming considerations related to the following tests:

- Cycle ergometer tests
  - ✓ YMCA bike test
- Ventilatory threshold tests
  - ✓ Submaximal talk test for first ventilatory threshold (VT1)
  - ✓ Lactate threshold testing [second ventilatory threshold (VT2)]
- Field tests
  - ✓ Rockport fitness walking test (1 mile)
  - ✓ 1.5-mile run test
- Step tests
  - ✓ YMCA submaximal step test

MUSCULAR FITNESS TESTING

For the safe and effective administration of physical fitness tests, a personal trainer should have knowledge of the following concepts related to muscular fitness testing:

- Appropriate use of, and reasons for, administering muscular fitness tests
- Muscular strength versus muscular endurance
- Health-related benefits of muscular fitness

Muscular Endurance Testing

A personal trainer should have a general understanding of the appropriate use of, protocol for, and programming considerations related to the following muscular endurance tests:

- Push-up test
- Curl-up test
- Body-weight squat test

Muscular Strength Testing

A personal trainer should have a general understanding of the appropriate use of, protocol for, and programming considerations related to the following muscular strength tests:

- 1-RM bench-press test
- 1-RM leg-press test
- 1-RM squat test
- Submaximal strength tests

SPORT-SKILL ASSESSMENTS

For the safe and effective administration of physical fitness tests, a personal trainer should have knowledge of the appropriate use of, and reasons for administering, sports-skill tests.

Power Testing: Field Tests

A personal trainer should have a general understanding of the appropriate use of, protocol for, and programming considerations related to the following field power tests:

- Anaerobic power
  - ✓ Standing long jump test
  - ✓ Vertical jump test

Speed, Agility, and Quickness Testing

A personal trainer should have a general understanding of the appropriate use of, protocol for, and programming considerations related to the following field speed, agility, and quickness tests:

- Pro agility test
- 40-yard dash

FITNESS TESTING ACCURACY

Personal trainers should be familiar with the various causes of fitness test inaccuracy, including:

- Client (test subject)
- Trainer or test technician
- Equipment
- Environment

GETTING STARTED

This chapter covers the various physiological assessments that a personal trainer must be able to perform and interpret in order to create safe and effective exercise programs for clients. After completing this chapter, you will have a better understanding of:

- Body-composition assessments and anthropometric measurements
- Cardiorespiratory fitness assessments, including ventilatory threshold testing and field testing
- Muscular-strength and muscular-endurance testing
- Sports-skill assessments, including tests of power, speed, agility, and quickness

REVIEW QUESTIONS

1. Which of the following identifiable signs or symptoms that merit immediate test termination and possible referral to a qualified healthcare professional is related to poor perfusion?
   A. Claudication
   B. Cyanosis
   C. Fatigue
   D. Ataxia

2. Individuals who are short in stature may not be good candidates for which type of testing?
   A. Cycle ergometer tests
   B. Treadmill tests
   C. Ventilatory threshold tests
   D. Step tests

3. Which of the following cardiorespiratory fitness tests uses the immediate post-recovery heart rate to assess a client's fitness level?
   A. First ventilatory threshold test
   B. Rockport fitness walking test
   C. YMCA bike test
   D. YMCA submaximal step test

4. According a report by Foster and Porcari, the risk of heart attack and sudden cardiac death during exercise among fitness facility members is _____ that of cardiac patients in a supervised rehabilitation program.
   A. Double
   B. Triple
   C. Five times
   D. 10 times

5. A male client who weighs 190 pounds has a one-repetition maximum of 225 pounds on the bench press exercise. His relative strength for this exercise is

   _____.
   A. 225 pounds
   B. 0.84
   C. 35 pounds
   D. 1.18

6. A competitive soccer player, whose sport requires an ability to accelerate, decelerate, change direction, and then accelerate again, is interested in completing an assessment to serve as a baseline against which he can measure future improvements. Which test will **BEST** measure these sports skills?
   A. YMCA bike test
   B. 40-yard dash
   C. Pro agility test
   D. 1.5-mile run test

7. Which response would warrant immediate termination of exercise testing?
   A. Ratings of perceived exertion (RPE) >14 (6 to 20 scale)
   B. Heart rate (HR) >age-predicted maximum
   C. Systolic blood pressure (SBP) >220 mmHg
   D. Diastolic blood pressure (DBP) >115 mmHg

8. Which body-composition assessment method produces percent fat estimates that can vary greatly from day to day based on the hydration status of the client being tested?
   A. Skinfolds
   B. Bioelectrical impedance analysis (BIA)
   C. Hydrostatic weighing
   D. Dual energy x-ray absorptiometry (DEXA)

9. You are working with a client who weighs 180 lb (82 kg) with a body-fat percentage of 20%. What will his approximate weight be when he reaches his goal of 15% body fat, assuming that his lean body mass remains constant?
   A. 144 lb (65 kg)
   B. 149 lb (68 kg)
   C. 169 lb (77 kg)
   D. 175 lb (80 kg)

10. Which assessment does **NOT** use predicted maximal heart rate or predicted $\dot{V}O_2max$, but instead provides an actual measured heart rate that corresponds to the client's unique metabolic response to exercise?
    A. YMCA bike test
    B. Bruce submaximal treadmill test
    C. Submaximal talk test for VT1
    D. Rockport fitness walking test

11. Which assessment would be **MOST** appropriate for a 54-year-old male client who has no contraindications for exercise but has not been regularly active in more than 10 years?
    A. 1.5-mile run test
    B. Rockport fitness walking test
    C. VT2 threshold test
    D. 1-RM leg-press test

12. Which of the responses represents the predicted one-repetition maximum (1-RM) bench press for a client who can perform 10 repetitions of the exercise with 150 lb (68 kg) with good form?
    A. 188 lb (85 kg)
    B. 200 lb (91 kg)
    C. 214 lb (97 kg)
    D. 224 lb (102 kg)

13. Which of the following is the **BEST** tool for assessing lower-body muscular strength?
    A. Body-weight squat test
    B. 10-RM leg press test
    C. Standing long jump test
    D. 1-RM squat test

14. When preparing a client for a one-repetition maximum (1-RM) strength test, what percentage of the client's estimated 1-RM should the personal trainer encourage the client to use during the first warm-up set?
    A. 25%
    B. 50%
    C. 75%
    D. 90%

15. For which of the following sports would an assessment of vertical jump height be **LEAST** useful?
    A. Basketball
    B. Volleyball
    C. Sprinting
    D. Football

16. Which of the following tests measures an individual's ability to accelerate, decelerate, change direction, and then accelerate again?
    A. 40-yard dash
    B. Pro-agility test
    C. Ladder drill
    D. 1.5-mile run test

ANSWER KEY

1. B. Cyanosis

Signs of poor perfusion include: lightheadedness, pallor (pale skin), cyanosis (bluish coloration, especially around the mouth), nausea, or cold and clammy skin.
ACE Personal Trainer Manual, 5th Edition, p. 196

2. D. Step tests

Individuals who are short in stature are not good candidates for step testing, as they may have trouble with the step height.
ACE Personal Trainer Manual, 5th Edition, p. 230

3. D. YMCA submaximal step test

In step tests, fitness level is determined by the immediate post-exercise recovery heart rate (HR). In essence, the *lower* the exercising or recovery HR, the *higher* the level of fitness.
ACE Personal Trainer Manual, 5th Edition, p. 230

4. B. Triple

The risk of heart attack and sudden cardiac death during exercise among fitness facility members is three times that of cardiac patients in a supervised rehabilitation program (Foster & Porcari, 2001). The risk can be reduced with appropriate pre-exercise screening and careful observation of clients during and following exercise.
ACE Personal Trainer Manual, 5th Edition, p. 213

5. D. 1.18

Relative strength is the maximal force a person is able to exert in relation to his or her body weight and is calculated using the formula: Relative strength = Absolute strength/Body weight, where absolute strength is defined as the one-repetition maximum. In this case, relative strength = 225 pounds/190 pounds = 1.18
ACE Personal Trainer Manual, 5th Edition, p. 240

6. C. Pro agility test

The pro agility test quickly and simply measures an individual's ability to accelerate, decelerate, change direction, and then accelerate again. In fact, the National Football League and USA Women's Soccer Team use this assessment as part of their battery of tests.
ACE Personal Trainer Manual, 5th Edition, p. 253

7. D. Diastolic blood pressure (DBP) >115 mmHg

During the administration of any exercise test involving exertion (e.g., cardiovascular or muscular endurance and/or strength test), trainers must always be aware of identifiable signs or symptoms that merit immediate test termination and possible referral to a qualified healthcare professional, including a significant drop (>10 mmHg) in systolic blood pressure (SBP) despite an increase in exercise intensity or an excessive rise in blood pressure (BP): SBP reaches >250 mmHg or diastolic blood pressure (DBP) reaches >115 mmHg.
ACE Personal Trainer Manual, 5th Edition, p. 195–196

8. B. Bioelectrical impedance analysis (BIA)

Optimal hydration is necessary for accurate results from BIA; thus, it can be difficult to account for a client's level of hydration at the time of testing.
ACE Personal Trainer Manual, 5th Edition, p. 198

9. C. 169 lb (77 kg)

100% − 20.0 = 80%
180 pounds x 0.80 = 144 pounds (65 kg)
100% − 15% = 85%
144/0.85 = 169 pounds (77 kg)
ACE Personal Trainer Manual, 5th ed., p. 206

10. C. Submaximal talk test for VT1

The objectives of the submaximal talk test for VT1 are to measure the HR response at VT1 by progressively increasing exercise intensity and achieving steady-state at each stage, as well as to identify the HR where the ability to talk continuously becomes compromised. This point represents the intensity where the individual can continue to talk while breathing with minimal discomfort and reflects an associated increase in tidal volume that should not compromise breathing rate or the ability to talk.
ACE Personal Trainer Manual, 5th Edition, p. 222–223

11. B. Rockport fitness walking test

The Rockport fitness walking test is suitable for many individuals, is easy to administer, and inexpensive to conduct. It is a good option for clients who have not been regularly physically active.
ACE Personal Trainer Manual, 5th Edition, p. 227

12. B. 200 lb (91 kg)

10 repetitions represents 75% of predicted 1-RM, therefore 150 lb (68 kg)/0.75 = 200 lb (91 kg).
ACE Personal Trainer Manual, 5th Edition, p. 243

13. D. 1-RM squat test

The 1-RM squat test is the only test in the provided responses that assesses lower-extremity strength.
ACE Personal Trainer Manual, 5th Edition, p. 240

14. B. 50%

The client should warm up with one set of light resistance (~50% of anticipated 1-RM weight) that allows five to 10 repetitions, and then rest for one minute.
ACE Personal Trainer Manual, 5th Edition, p. 242, 245, & 247

15. C. Sprinting

The vertical jump test is especially valuable when assessing the vertical jump height in athletes who participate in sports that require skill and power in jumping (e.g., basketball, volleyball, or football). While sprinting is a powerful endeavor, the focus is on propelling oneself more horizontal than vertical.
ACE Personal Trainer Manual, 5th Edition, p. 252

16. B. Pro-agility test

The pro agility test is sometimes called the 20-yard agility test or the 5-10-5 shuttle run. This test quickly and simply measures an individual's ability to accelerate, decelerate, change direction, and then accelerate again.
ACE Personal Trainer Manual, 5th Edition, p. 253

FUNCTIONAL PROGRAMMING
FOR STABILITY-MOBILITY AND MOVEMENT

READING ASSIGNMENT

You should now have completed the reading of Chapter 9 of the *ACE Personal Trainer Manual,* 5th Edition. Carefully review the Summary Review below, as this content highlights valuable information that is particularly relevant to fitness professionals, both in importance and frequency of application or occurrence in the practice of personal training.

Then, answer the Chapter 9 Review Questions and check your answers using the corresponding Answer Key. Review the section in the *ACE Personal Trainer Manual,* 5th Edition, associated with any questions you may have missed.

SUMMARY REVIEW

Knowledge of the following terms and concepts related to human movement is essential for all personal trainers:
- Joint mobility versus joint stability
- Factors contributing to movement efficiency
- Movement compensations associated with typical mobility problems
- Length-tension relationships
- Force-couple relationships
- Neural control

PHASE 1: STABILITY AND MOBILITY TRAINING

A personal trainer should have knowledge of the following terms and concepts related to the first phase of functional exercise programming:
- Contributions of slow-twitch and fast-twitch muscle fibers to joint stability and mobility
- Stretching techniques during each phase of a workout session
  - ✓ Self–myofascial release
  - ✓ Static stretches
  - ✓ Proprioceptive neuromuscular facilitation (PNF)
  - ✓ Dynamic and ballistic stretches
- Proximal stability: activating the core
  - ✓ Contribution of each layer of core musculature to spinal stability and mobility
  - ✓ Three-stage model for core and balance training
- Proximal stability: core function
  - ✓ Exercise progression for core activation
  - ✓ Supine drawing-in (centering) exercise
  - ✓ Quadruped drawing-in (centering) with extremity movement exercise
- Proximal mobility: hips and thoracic spine
  - ✓ Fundamental programming principles to improve mobility in the hips and thoracic spine
  - ✓ Exercise progression for core stabilization

✓ Exercises and stretches (and their progressions) to promote mobility in the hips and thoracic spine
- Proximal stability of the scapulothoracic region and distal mobility of the glenohumeral joint
  ✓ Exercises and stretches (and their progressions) to promote function in the scapulothoracic region and the glenohumeral joint
- Distal mobility
- Static balance
  ✓ Training guidelines for static balance
  ✓ Specific static-balance exercises and their progressions
- Dynamic balance
- Single-leg patterns

PHASE 2: MOVEMENT TRAINING

A personal trainer should have knowledge of the following terms and concepts related to the second phase of functional exercise programming:
- The five primary movements that encompass all activities of daily living (ADL)
- The importance of incorporating the five primary movements into a client's exercise programming
- The contribution of "glute dominance," "quad dominance," and "lumbar dominance" to human movement patterns
- Exercises and stretches (and their progressions) that train the five primary movement patterns
  ✓ Bend-and-lift patterns
  ✓ Single-leg stand patterns
  ✓ Pushing movements
  ✓ Pulling movements
  ✓ Rotational movements
- Dynamic movement patterns over a static base of support

GETTING STARTED

This chapter covers phases 1 and 2 of the functional movement and resistance-training component of the ACE Integrated Fitness Training® (ACE IFT®) Model—stability and mobility training and movement training. After completing this chapter, you will have a better understanding of:
- Length-tension and force-couple relationships
- The various components of stability and mobility training, including core function, proximal mobility and stability, distal mobility, and static and dynamic balance
- The five primary patterns of movement training—bend-and-lift patterns, single-leg stand patterns, pushing movements, pulling movements, and rotational movements—and how they are addressed in the movement-training phase

REVIEW QUESTIONS

1. Which of the following joints is classified as favoring stability over mobility?
   A. Scapulothoracic
   B. Ankle
   C. Thoracic spine
   D. Glenohumeral

2. A lack of hip joint mobility is **MOST** likely to lead to which of the following?
   A. Hypermobility in the scapulothoracic joints and thoracic spine
   B. Compromised stability in the knees and lumbar spine
   C. Hypermobility in the knee, ankle, and foot joints
   D. Compromised mobility in the knees and lumbar spine

3. Limited movement over an extended period of time, such as is seen with injury and postural deviations, can result in muscle shortening on one side of a joint and muscle lengthening on the other side of the joint. How do these length changes affect the force-generating capacity of these muscles?
   A. The lengthened muscles generally have a higher force production throughout the full range of motion, as muscles are strongest when they are longest.
   B. The shortened muscles will produce the same amount of force as they did at normal length, only at a faster rate of movement.
   C. They will have greater force-generating capacity at their new lengths, but diminished force-generating capacity at normal resting lengths.
   D. They will have diminished force-generating capacity at their new lengths, but greater force-generating capacity at normal resting lengths.

4. Which force couple creates posterior pelvic rotation to pull the pelvis out of anterior pelvic tilt?
   A. Hip flexors and erector spinae
   B. Hamstrings and erector spinae
   C. Hip flexors and rectus abdominis
   D. Hamstrings and rectus abdominis

5. The middle layer of torso muscles that are commonly referred to as "the core" consists of the _____.
   A. Multifidi, quadratus lumborum, transverse abdominis, deep fibers of the internal oblique, diaphragm, and pelvic floor musculature
   B. Erector spinae, external oblique, deep fibers of the internal oblique, iliopsoas, rectus abdominis, and latissimus dorsi
   C. Transverse abdominis, diaphragm, interspinali, intertransversarii, and rotatores
   D. Quadratus lumborum, multifidi, external oblique, erector spinae, and pelvic floor musculature

6. Once a client can perform two sets of 10 repetitions of glute bridges, which exercise would provide the **MOST** appropriate progression?
   A. Single-leg glute bridge with a riser under the thoracic spine
   B. Stability ball single-leg glute bridge with opposite knee to chest
   C. Single-leg glute bridge with opposite knee to chest
   D. Stability ball single-leg glute bridge with opposite leg straight

7. When helping a client build scapulothoracic stability, which exercise should a trainer have him or her perform **FIRST** to teach the client how to "pack" the scapula?
   A. Shoulder diagonals without resistance
   B. Supine shoulder depression and shoulder retraction
   C. Prone arm lifts in "I," "Y," "W," and "O" formations
   D. Supine shoulder internal and external rotation with tubing

8. Once a client can demonstrate good static balance while standing on two feet, what exercise could the trainer introduce that would provide the **MOST** appropriate progression?
   A. Reducing points of contact (two feet to one foot)
   B. Balancing on an unstable surface
   C. Raising arms overhead with eyes closed
   D. Narrowing the base of support

9. Which progression follows the part-to-whole teaching strategy in helping a client learn proper technique for the bend-and-lift squatting movement?

   A. Hip hinge, lower extremity alignment, figure-4 position

   B. Figure-4 position, squats with varied foot position, lunges

   C. Hip hinge, figure-4 position, squats with varied foot positions, squats with arm drivers

   D. Figure-4 position, squats with arm drivers, lunge matrix

10. Once a client demonstrates good form while performing kneeling wood-chop spiral patterns with short and long moment arms, what exercise would provide the **MOST** appropriate progression?

    A. Standing wood-chops and hay balers with full rotation

    B. Standing wood-chops and hay balers with long moment arms

    C. Standing wood-chops and hay balers with 2-kg medicine ball

    D. Standing wood-chop spiral patterns with short moment arms

11. Muscles have been shown to shorten when held passively in shortened positions in as few as

    _____.

    A. Two to four hours

    B. Two to three days

    C. Two to four weeks

    D. Two to three months

12. Which of the following neuromuscular principles occurs when the activation of a muscle on one side of a joint coincides with neural inhibition of the opposing muscle on the other side of the joint?

    A. Reciprocal inhibition

    B. Autogenic inhibition

    C. Stress relaxation

    D. Stretch shortening

13. Which muscle group is primarily responsible for the "hoop tension" effect during core stabilization techniques?

    A. Rectus abdominis

    B. External obliques

    C. Transverse abdominis

    D. Multifidi

ANSWER KEY

1. A. Scapulothoracic

The scapulothoracic joint favors stability over mobility and, when functioning properly, provides a stable base for movements of the glenohumeral joint.
ACE Personal Trainer Manual, 5th Edition, p. 264

2. B. Compromised stability in the knees and lumbar spine

When hip mobility is limited, adjacent, more stable joints may need to compromise some degree of stability to facilitate the level of mobility needed (e.g., the knee and lumbar spine).
ACE Personal Trainer Manual, 5th Edition, p. 264–265

3. C. They will have greater force-generating capacity at their new lengths, but diminished force-generating capacity at normal resting lengths.

Due to the muscles undergoing an adaptive change in sarcomeres in series, they will have greater force-generating capacity at their new lengths, but diminished force-generating capacity at normal resting lengths.
ACE Personal Trainer Manual, 5th Edition, p. 266–267

4. D. Hamstrings and rectus abdominis

Maintenance of a neutral pelvic position is achieved via opposing force-couples between four major muscle groups that all have attachments on the pelvis. The rectus abdominis pulls upward on the anterior, inferior pelvis, while the hip flexors pull downward on the anterior, superior pelvis. On the posterior surface, the hamstrings pull downward on the posterior, inferior pelvis, while the erector spinae pull upward on the posterior, superior pelvis.
ACE Personal Trainer Manual, 5th Edition, p. 267–286

5. A. Multifidi, quadratus lumborum, transverse abdominis, deep fibers of the internal oblique, diaphragm, and pelvic floor musculature

The transverse abdominis (TVA), multifidi, quadratus lumborum, deep fibers of the internal oblique, diaphragm, pelvic floor musculature, and the adjoining fasciae (linea alba and thoracolumbar fascia) make up the muscular layer usually referred to as the core.
ACE Personal Trainer Manual, 5th Edition, p. 275–276

6. C. Single-leg glute bridge with opposite knee to chest

A single-leg glute bridge with opposite knee to chest is the next appropriate progression because it keeps the body on a stable surface (i.e., the floor) while challenging the core and placing more emphasis on one set of gluteals.
ACE Personal Trainer Manual, 5th Edition, p. 286

7. B. Supine shoulder depression and shoulder retraction

To kinesthetically improve awareness of good scapular position, improving flexibility and strength of key parascapular muscles, the first exercise clients should perform is supine shoulder depression and shoulder retraction.
ACE Personal Trainer Manual, 5th Edition, p. 292

8. D. Narrowing the base of support

A person's center of mass (COM) constantly shifts as he or she changes position, moves, or adds external resistance. Base of support (BOS) is defined as the two-dimensional distance between and beneath the body's points of contact with a surface. Moving the feet closer together reduces this area, and consequently the BOS, thereby reducing balance control. From a normal standing position, narrowing the BOS is the first progression for challenging balance.
ACE Personal Trainer Manual, 5th Edition, p. 298 & 300–301

9. A. Hip hinge, lower extremity alignment, figure-4 position

The hip hinge, lower-extremity alignment, and figure-4 position is the proper part-to-whole strategy when teaching a client to squat.
ACE Personal Trainer Manual, 5th Edition, p. 308–309

10. D. Standing wood-chop spiral patterns with short moment arms

The next appropriate progression is to introduce standing wood-chop spiral patterns with short moment arms because it reduces the base of support without adding other stability and mobility challenges.
ACE Personal Trainer Manual, 5th Edition, p. 320

11. C. Two to four weeks

Muscles can shorten in as little as two to four weeks when held in passively shortened positions without being stretched or used through a full or functional ROM (e.g., continuous bouts of sitting hunched over a desk without extension activity within the upper thorax can shorten the pectoralis major).
ACE Personal Trainer Manual, 5th Edition, p. 266

12. A. Reciprocal inhibition

Reciprocal inhibition is the principle stating that activation of a muscle on one side of a joint (i.e., the agonist) coincides with neural inhibition of the opposing muscle on the other side of the joint (i.e., the antagonist) to facilitate movement.
ACE Personal Trainer Manual, 5th Edition, p. 272

13. C. Transverse abdominis

Activation of the core muscles, primarily the transverse abdominis, produces a "hoop tension" effect similar to that of cinching a belt around the waist.
ACE Personal Trainer Manual, 5th Edition, p. 276

RESISTANCE TRAINING:
PROGRAMMING AND PROGRESSIONS

 READING ASSIGNMENT

You should now have completed the reading of Chapter 10 of the *ACE Personal Trainer Manual,* 5th Edition. Carefully review the Summary Review below, as this content highlights valuable information that is particularly relevant to fitness professionals, both in importance and frequency of application or occurrence in the practice of personal training.

Then, answer the Chapter 10 Review Questions and check your answers using the corresponding Answer Key. Review the section in the *ACE Personal Trainer Manual,* 5th Edition, associated with any questions you may have missed.

SUMMARY REVIEW

BENEFITS OF RESISTANCE TRAINING

Personal trainers should understand the positive impact of resistance training for clients, including the following benefits:

- Increased physical capacity
- Improved physical appearance and body composition
- Enhanced metabolic function
- Decreased injury risk and enhanced disease prevention

PHYSIOLOGICAL ADAPTATIONS TO RESISTANCE TRAINING: ACUTE AND LONG-TERM

It is important that personal trainers are familiar with the terms and concepts related to the following physiological adaptations to resistance training:

- Acute adaptations in the nervous and endocrine systems during a resistance-training workout
- Long-term physiological adaptations to progressive resistance exercise (i.e., increased muscle strength and hypertrophy)
- Factors that influence muscle strength and hypertrophy
  - ✓ Hormone levels
  - ✓ Sex
  - ✓ Age
  - ✓ Muscle fiber type
  - ✓ Muscle length
  - ✓ Limb length
  - ✓ Tendon insertion point

MUSCULAR STRENGTH/POWER/ENDURANCE RELATIONSHIPS

A personal trainer should be familiar with the following terms and concepts related to muscular strength, power, and endurance:

- Muscular strength versus muscular endurance
- One-repetition maximum (1-RM)
- Muscular power
- Relationship between exercise weightload and muscular power

TRAINING VARIABLES: FACTORS AFFECTING STRENGTH DEVELOPMENT AND PROGRAM DESIGN

A personal trainer should be familiar with the following terms and concepts related to the development of a strength-training program:

- Client needs assessment
  - ✓ Health- and skill-related parameters
- Training frequency
- Exercise selection and order
- Training volume
- Appropriate program progressions
- Training intensity
- Training tempo
- Rest intervals

TRAINING PRINCIPLES

A personal trainer should be familiar with the following resistance-training principles:

- Progression
- Specificity
- Overload
- Reversibility
- Diminishing returns

RESISTANCE-TRAINING PERIODIZATION MODELS

A personal trainer should be familiar with the following terms and concepts related to resistance-training periodization models:

- Macrocycles
- Mesocycles
- Microcycles
- Linear versus undulating periodization

PROGRAM DESIGN USING THE ACE INTEGRATED FITNESS TRAINING® MODEL

For safe and effective resistance-training program design, a personal trainer should be familiar with the following terms, concepts, and appropriate rates of progression related to the ACE Integrated Fitness Training (ACE IFT®) Model:

- Phase 1: Stability and mobility training
- Phase 2: Movement training
- Phase 3: Load training
  - ✓ Programming comparisons for general health and fitness, strength, and hypertrophy
- Phase 4: Performance training
  - ✓ Client prerequisites for performance training
  - ✓ Plyometrics
  - ✓ Speed, power, and agility

SMALL-GROUP TRAINING

As more and more fitness professionals are getting into the practice of seeing clients in a small-group setting, it is important for personal trainers to understand the following concepts related to programming for clients in the small-group setting:

- Benefits of group participation
- Group homogeneity
- Recognizing the need for personal attention

SPECIAL CONSIDERATIONS FOR YOUTH AND OLDER ADULTS

Personal trainers should understand the following factors as they relate to resistance training for youth and older adults:

- Youth strength training
  - ✓ Benefits of strength training in youth
  - ✓ National Strength and Conditioning Association (NSCA) guidelines for youth resistance training

- Older adult strength training
  - ✓ Benefits of strength training in older adults
  - ✓ Exercise precautions and guidelines for older adults

STRENGTH TRAINING EQUIPMENT OPTIONS

The types of, and appropriate uses for, the following categories of exercise equipment should be understood by all personal trainers:

- Selectorized equipment
- Cables
- Free weights
- Tubing
- Medicine balls
- Body-weight training

ERGOGENIC AIDS AND SUPPLEMENTS

A personal trainer should have basic knowledge of the impact on performance and health-related consequences of consuming the following ergogenic aids and supplements:

- Protein and amino-acid supplements
- β-Alanine (carnosine) and sodium bicarbonate
- Caffeine
- Creatine
- Performance-optimizing vitamins and minerals
- Anabolic-androgenic steroids and related compounds

COMMON RESISTANCE-TRAINING MYTHS AND MISTAKES

Personal trainers should have a good understanding of the following common resistance-training myths and mistakes in order to educate their clients about the proper applications and outcomes of regular resistance training:

- "Fat deposits in certain areas can be targeted with strength training via spot reduction."
- "Women will build bulky muscles through weight training."
- "Individuals should use light weights and high repetitions to improve muscle tone, and heavy weights and low repetitions to increase muscle mass."
- "At some point, people get too old to lift weights."
- "Children are too young to lift weights."
- "Free weights are always better than machines."
- "After a person stops resistance training, the muscle turns to fat."
- "Strength training is bad for the exerciser's blood pressure."

GETTING STARTED

This chapter begins by discussing the benefits and acute and long-term physiological adaptations to resistance training. It also covers the resistance-training component of the ACE IFT Model, specifically focusing on phases 3 and 4—load training and performance training. After completing this chapter, you will have a better understanding of:

- The various training variables, including frequency, intensity, and rest intervals
- Training principles, including overload, progression, and specificity
- Both linear and undulating periodization programs
- Strength-training equipment options
- Ergogenic aids and supplements

REVIEW QUESTIONS

1. Which of the following physiological states would **MOST** likely occur as a result of one resistance-training session?
   A. Increased strength
   B. Transient hypertrophy
   C. Bone remodeling
   D. Increased lean body mass

2. Your new client is a 47-year-old woman who wants to lose weight, but is a bit apprehensive about resistance training because she does not want to "get big." Based on this information, what response would **BEST** facilitate resistance-training program adherence and motivation?
   A. Design a program based primarily on cardiorespiratory exercise with a light (40% 1-RM) circuit with high-repetition (15–25) sets to help her comfortably meet her goals.
   B. Tell her that she has nothing to worry about, as women do not produce enough of the male hormone testosterone to "get big."
   C. Show empathy for her concern about getting big and ensure her that you will design a program that will help her to get toned without getting big.
   D. Explain the average adult muscle-tissue loss of 5 lb (2.3 kg) per decade, and how resistance training can help her restore lost muscle and raise resting metabolism.

3. Which of the following statements about the role of type I muscle fibers during resistance-training exercises is **MOST** accurate?
   A. They are responsible for producing quick, high-force movements
   B. They are active primarily during lower levels of force production
   C. They are oxidative and not active during resistance exercises
   D. They are only active when performing 15 or more repetitions

4. Performing which combination of sets, repetitions, and load would result in the **GREATEST** total training volume?
   A. 2 sets x 8 repetitions with 100 pounds (45.5 kg)
   B. 1 set x 12 repetitions with 150 pounds (68.2 kg)
   C. 3 sets x 4 repetitions with 160 pounds (90.9 kg)
   D. 2 sets x 12 repetitions with 90 pounds (40.9 kg)

5. You are working with a new client who wants to begin resistance training in preparation for a one-month backpacking trip he will be taking through the Rocky Mountains. Which of the following training sets and repetition ranges would be **BEST** for helping him prepare for the rigors of this multiday trip?
   A. 1–2 sets of 8–10 repetitions
   B. 2–4 sets of 4–6 repetitions
   C. 2–3 sets of 12–16 repetitions
   D. 3–5 sets of 6–12 repetitions

6. What work-to-recovery ratio would be **MOST** appropriate to include in a resistance-training circuit for small-group personal-training sessions with clients who have primary goals that require enhanced muscular endurance?
   A. 75-second work interval:15-second recovery interval
   B. 90-second work interval:2–3 minute recovery interval
   C. 90-second work interval:60-second recovery interval
   D. 75-second work interval:3–5 minute recovery interval

7. The resistance-training program you have designed for a client has her performing 8–12 repetitions during each set, using a double-progressive training protocol for advancing workload. During her most recent personal-training session, she was able to perform two sets of 12 repetitions on the leg press machine with 200 lb (90.9 kg). Based on this information, what would be the **MOST** appropriate progression for her on the leg press exercise?

    A. Increase weight to 220 lb (100 kg) and work toward 12 repetitions at this new weight

    B. Continue with current weight until reaching 15 repetitions per set, then increase weight by 10%

    C. Increase weight to 210 lb (95.5 kg) and work toward 12 repetitions at this new weight

    D. Raise the weight to 240 lb (109.1 kg) and perform eight repetitions

8. Which of the following programs would be **MOST** appropriate for a client who has a primary focus on improving muscular strength?

    A. Two sets of 4–6 repetitions for each major muscle group or movement pattern, utilizing a split routine that allows 72–96 hours of recovery time before working the same muscle group again

    B. Two sets of 8–12 repetitions for each major movement pattern, utilizing a three-day undulating periodization model for full-body training with 48 hours of recovery time between workouts

    C. Three sets of 8–10 repetitions for each major muscle group or movement pattern, utilizing a split routine that allows 48–72 hours of recovery time before working the same muscle group again

    D. Three sets of 3–5 repetitions on explosive, full-body exercises performed 3 days per week with 48–72 hours of recovery time between workouts

9. You are working with a client who wants to train for a specific athletic competition. Before progressing this client to performance training (phase 4), what criteria should he meet to allow for a safe and effective transition to this type of training?

    A. Successful completion of stability and mobility training followed by 12 weeks of load training

    B. Good postural stability, proper movement patterns, and relatively high levels of strength

    C. Successful completion of stability and mobility training and movement training

    D. Regular participation in resistance training for at least three consecutive years

10. What plyometric drill would provide the **MOST** appropriate progression for a client who can successfully perform a predetermined number of vertical jumps and single linear jumps?

    A. Depth jumps

    B. Multidirectional jumps

    C. Hops and bounds

    D. Multiple linear jumps

11. Which of the following groups of individuals would work **BEST** together in a small-group training session?

    A. Four people with similar fitness goals

    B. Three people at various levels of fitness

    C. Five people with similar orthopedic problems

    D. Four people who can commit to the program based on schedule availability

ANSWER KEY

1. B. Transient hypertrophy

Transient hypertrophy, a term denoting the "muscle pump" experienced by many people immediately following resistance training, is caused by fluid accumulation in the spaces between cells (due to muscle contraction) and it quickly diminishes after exercise as the fluid balance between the various tissues and compartments returns to normal.
ACE Personal Trainer Manual, 5th Edition, p. 331

2. D. Explain the average adult muscle-tissue loss of 5 lb (2.3 kg) per decade, and how resistance training can help her restore lost muscle and raise resting metabolism

On average, previously untrained adults may increase their muscle mass by 1.4 kg, increase resting metabolic rate (RMR) by 7%, and reduce fat weight by 1.8 kg after 10 weeks of resistance training. Explaining these facts related to weight loss can help clients appreciate weight training's role in a comprehensive exercise program.
ACE Personal Trainer Manual, 5th Edition, p. 327

3. B. They are active primarily during lower levels of force production

Type I fibers are typically smaller with more aerobic power (lower levels of force production for longer periods of time), whereas type II fibers are typically larger with more anaerobic capacity (higher levels of force production for shorter periods of time).
ACE Personal Trainer Manual, 5th Edition, p. 332

4. D. 2 sets x 12 repetitions with 90 pounds (40.9 kg)

Using the load-volume calculation (volume = exercise weightload x repetitions x sets), 2 sets x 12 repetitions with 90 pounds (40.9 kg) = 2,160 pounds, which is the highest volume response option listed.
ACE Personal Trainer Manual, 5th Edition, p. 337–338

5. C. 2–3 sets of 12–16 repetitions

2–3 sets of 12–16 repetitions is an endurance-focused program, which would be the most supportive of a client who wants to train for a hiking trip.
ACE Personal Trainer Manual, 5th Edition, p. 338

6. A. 75-second work interval:15-second recovery interval

An interval routine that includes a 75-second work interval and a 15-second recovery interval fits within the muscular-endurance training parameters of ≥12 repetitions and ≤30 seconds rest.
ACE Personal Trainer Manual, 5th Edition, p. 338

7. C. Increase weight to 210 lb (95.5 kg) and work toward 12 repetitions at this new weight

In the double-progressive strength-training protocol, the first progression is adding repetitions, and the second progression is adding resistance in approximately 5% increments.
ACE Personal Trainer Manual, 5th Edition, p. 341

8. A. Two sets of 4–6 repetitions for each major muscle group or movement pattern, utilizing a split routine that allows 72–96 hours of recovery time before working the same muscle group again

For muscular strength optimization, clients should train at an intensity (load) that fatigues the targeted muscle groups at 4 to 8 repetitions per set and allows at least 72 hours of recovery between working the same muscle group subsequently.
ACE Personal Trainer Manual, 5th Edition, p. 353

9. B. Good postural stability, proper movement patterns, and relatively high levels of strength

To ensure program safety and success, clients with athletic performance goals should have the following prerequisites:
- A foundation of strength and joint integrity (joint mobility and stability)
- Adequate static and dynamic balance
- Effective core function
- Anaerobic efficiency (training of the anaerobic pathways)
- Athleticism (sufficient skills to perform advanced movements)
- No contraindications to load-bearing, dynamic movements
- No medical concerns that affect balance and motor skills

ACE Personal Trainer Manual, 5th Edition, p. 359–360

10. D. Multiple linear jumps

The most appropriate progression in this case is to increase the number of linear jumps by stringing several together consecutively, thereby creating multiple linear jumps.
ACE Personal Trainer Manual, 5th Edition, p. 364

11. A. Four people with similar fitness goals

Clients with similar fitness goals work better together in a group. For example, an athlete who is interested in increasing his or her vertical jump height through plyometric training would not be a good match if paired with a middle-aged client concerned with lowering blood pressure and losing weight.
ACE Personal Trainer Manual, 5th Edition, p. 374

CARDIORESPIRATORY TRAINING:
PROGRAMMING AND PROGRESSIONS

 READING ASSIGNMENT

You should now have completed the reading of Chapter 11 of the *ACE Personal Trainer Manual,* 5th Edition. Carefully review the Summary Review below, as this content highlights valuable information that is particularly relevant to fitness professionals, both in importance and frequency of application or occurrence in the practice of personal training.

Then, answer the Chapter 11 Review Questions and check your answers using the corresponding Answer Key. Review the section in the *ACE Personal Trainer Manual,* 5th Edition, associated with any questions you may have missed.

SUMMARY REVIEW

PHYSIOLOGICAL ADAPTATIONS TO ACUTE AND CHRONIC CARDIORESPIRATORY EXERCISE

For safe and effective exercise programming, personal trainers must have knowledge of the fundamental physiological adaptations to cardiorespiratory exercise related to the following topic areas:

- Muscular system
- Cardiovascular system
- Respiratory system
- Time required for increases in aerobic power
- Physiological adaptations to steady-state and interval-based exercise

COMPONENTS OF A CARDIORESPIRATORY WORKOUT SESSION

A personal trainer should have knowledge of the concepts related to the following components of a cardiorespiratory workout session:

- Warm-up
- Conditioning phase
  ✓ Cardiovascular drift
- Cool-down

GENERAL GUIDELINES FOR CARDIORESPIRATORY EXERCISE FOR HEALTH, FITNESS, AND WEIGHT LOSS

A personal trainer should be familiar with the following terms and concepts related to cardiorespiratory exercise programming and understand the impact of each on a client's acute and long-term exercise performance:

- *2008 Physical Activity Guidelines for Americans* by the U.S. Department of Health & Human Services
- Physical-activity guidelines from the American College of Sports Medicine (ACSM) and the American Heart Association (AHA)

- Frequency
- Intensity
  - ✓ Cardiovascular recommendations for healthy adults
  - ✓ Recommended framework for exercise intensity for apparently healthy adults
- Heart rate
- Karvonen formula
- Ratings of perceived exertion (RPE)
- $\dot{V}O_2$ or metabolic equivalents
- First ventilatory threshold (VT1)
- Second ventilatory threshold (VT2)
- Caloric expenditure
- Talk test
- Blood lactate and VT2
  - ✓ Training zones (1 through 3)
- Duration
- Exercise progression
  - ✓ Recommendations for exercise duration and quantity
- Fartlek training

MODES OR TYPES OF CARDIORESPIRATORY EXERCISE

A personal trainer should be knowledgeable about the following terms and concepts related to modes of cardiorespiratory exercise and the appropriateness of each for individual clients:

- Physical activities that promote improvement or maintenance of cardiorespiratory fitness
- Equipment-based cardiovascular exercise
- Group exercise
- Circuit training
- Outdoor exercise
- Seasonal exercise
- Water-based exercise
- Mind-body exercise
- Lifestyle exercise

ACE INTEGRATED FITNESS TRAINING® MODEL—CARDIORESPIRATORY TRAINING PHASES

A personal trainer should have an understanding of the training focus and program-design considerations for each phase of the ACE Integrated Fitness Training (ACE IFT®) Model:

- Phase 1: Aerobic-base training
- Phase 2: Aerobic-efficiency training
- Phase 3: Anaerobic-endurance training
- Phase 4: Anaerobic-power training

RECOVERY AND REGENERATION

A personal trainer should be familiar with the concepts related to recovery and regeneration and understand the impact of each on a client's acute and long-term exercise performance.

SPECIAL CONSIDERATIONS FOR YOUTH AND OLDER ADULTS

A personal trainer should have an understanding of the following terms and concepts related to the unique training considerations for youth and older adults:
- Youth
  - ✓ Overspecialization
  - ✓ Orthopedic trauma
- Older adults
  - ✓ Cardiovascular risk
  - ✓ Orthopedic risk
  - ✓ Preservation of muscle tissue
  - ✓ The rate at which older individuals adapt to training

GETTING STARTED

This chapter features a discussion of the physiological adaptations to acute and chronic cardiorespiratory exercise. It also includes coverage of the cardiorespiratory-training phases of the ACE IFT Model. After completing this chapter, you will have a better understanding of:
- How cardiorespiratory exercise affects the following systems: muscular, cardiovascular, and respiratory
- The components of a well-designed cardiorespiratory-training session
- General guidelines for cardiorespiratory exercise
- Various modes of cardiorespiratory exercise
- Special considerations for youth and older adults

REVIEW QUESTIONS

1. When performing steady-state cardiorespiratory exercise, which of the following is **LEAST** likely to limit exercise duration?

    A. Availability of oxygen

    B. Availability of energy from stored fat and/or free fatty acids

    C. The willingness to continue

    D. Availability of energy from stored glycogen and/or blood glucose

2. What causes cardiovascular drift?

    A. Increased heart rate to compensate for reduced blood volume due to sweat production for thermoregulation

    B. Decreased heart rate resulting from an inability to sustain cardiac output due to fatigue

    C. Increased stroke volume to compensate for reduced blood volume due to sweat production for thermoregulation

    D. Decreased stroke volume resulting from an inability to sustain cardiac output due to fatigue

3. What is the **PRIMARY** reason for having all clients perform an adequate cool-down?

    A. To prevent delayed-onset muscle soreness (DOMS)

    B. To perform static stretching for enhanced flexibility

    C. To enhance venous return to prevent blood pooling in the extremities

    D. To maintain increased caloric expenditure to enhance weight loss

4. What is the **GREATEST** limitation associated with using heart-rate reserve (HRR) to calculate exercise target heart rate?

    A. Target heart rate must be calculated as a %HRR using the Karvonen formula

    B. Accurate programming using HRR requires actual measured maximal heart rate (MHR) and resting heart rate

    C. New MHR prediction equations are more accurate than MHR = 220 − age

    D. Exercise percentages were established through population-based research

5. Which of the following weekly training plans would have a session rating of perceived exertion (session RPE) of 450 points?

    A. 4 sessions x 25 minutes at an RPE of 5

    B. 2 sessions x 30 minutes at an RPE of 5 and 2 sessions x 20 minutes at an RPE of 3

    C. 3 sessions x 30 minutes at an RPE of 5

    D. 2 sessions x 30 minutes at an RPE of 4 and 3 sessions 20 minutes at an RPE of 4.5

6. During cardiorespiratory exercise with progressively increasing intensity, the need for additional oxygen is met initially through linear increases in minute ventilation ($\dot{V}_E$). The point at which the increased demands for oxygen can no longer be met by this linear increase, causing a nonlinear increase in ventilation is known as the _____ and can be measured via a

    _____.

    A. Aerobic power; $\dot{V}O_2$max test

    B. Second ventilatory threshold (VT2); VT2 threshold test

    C. Onset of blood lactate accumulation (OBLA); blood lactate analyzer

    D. First ventilatory threshold (VT1); submaximal talk test for VT1

7. Which of the following corresponds with the second ventilatory threshold (VT2)?

    A. Talk test threshold

    B. Onset of blood lactate accumulation (OBLA)

    C. Aerobic power

    D. The dividing point between zone 1 and zone 2

8. What is the **PRIMARY** focus of aerobic-base training in the ACE IFT Model?

    A. Creating positive experiences and early success through achievable zone 1 exercise of increasing duration

    B. Progressively increasing zone 2 intervals to intensities just below VT2

    C. Building a strong endurance base as part of a periodization plan for performance in long-distance events

    D. Transitioning from training for improved health to training for improved fitness

9. Most fitness enthusiasts who exercise in a gym or at home on a regular basis on multiple days per week will spend many years reaching their fitness goals through aerobic-efficiency training. Research with these well-trained non-athletes has found that they will spend as much as _____% of their total training time in zone 2.

    A. 10

    B. 25

    C. 35

    D. 50

10. Which of the following training scenarios would **MOST** likely result in overtraining syndrome for an endurance athlete?

    A. Increasing the intensity of zone 3 intervals by 10% from one week to the next

    B. Decreasing the number of recovery days per week to accommodate additional interval work

    C. Increasing the duration of zone 1 training by 20% over the course of three weeks

    D. Decreasing the total time spent doing zone 2 interval work when increasing the intensity

ANSWER KEY

1. B. Availability of energy from stored fat and/or free fatty acids

Exercise duration is primarily limited by the willingness to continue or by the availability of oxygen, muscle glycogen, and/or blood glucose.
ACE Personal Trainer Manual, 5th Edition, p. 395

2. A. Increased heart rate to compensate for reduced blood volume due to sweat production for thermoregulation

Causes for cardiovascular drift include the following:
- Small reductions in blood volume that occur during exercise due to fluid lost to sweat and fluid moving into the spaces between cells, which results in a compensatory increase in heart rate to maintain cardiac output, offsetting the small decrease in stroke volume (Cardiac output = Heart rate x Stroke volume)
- Increasing core temperature that directs greater quantities of blood to the skin to facilitate heat loss, consequently decreasing blood return to the heart and blood available for the exercising muscles
ACE Personal Trainer Manual, 5th Edition, p. 397

3. C. To enhance venous return to prevent blood pooling in the extremities

The cool-down phase is directed primarily toward preventing the tendency for blood to pool in the extremities, which may occur when exercise ends. The cessation of significant venous return from the "muscle pump" experienced during exercise can cause blood to accumulate in the lower extremity, reducing blood flow back to the heart and out to vital organs (e.g., the brain, potentially causing symptoms of lightheadedness).
ACE Personal Trainer Manual, 5th Edition, p. 398

4. B. Accurate programming using HRR requires actual measured maximal heart rate (MHR) and resting heart rate

The HRR model has limitations regarding its accuracy and appropriateness. There is some debate over the body position in which RHR is measured. The Karvonen formula was created measuring true resting heart rate (RHR), taken in the morning in a reclining position. Also, ideally, this technique should be based on measured maximal heart rate to yield the most accurate results.
ACE Personal Trainer Manual, 5th Edition, p. 402

5. C. 3 sessions x 30 minutes at an RPE of 5

3 sessions x 30 minutes = 90 minutes. Ninety minutes x an RPE of 5 = 450 points.
ACE Personal Trainer Manual, 5th Edition, p. 404

6. D. First ventilatory threshold (VT1); submaximal talk test for VT1

The submaximal talk test works on the premise that at about the intensity of VT1, the increase in ventilation is accomplished by an increase in breathing frequency. One of the requirements of comfortable speech is to be able to control breathing frequency. Thus, at the intensity of VT1, it is no longer possible to speak comfortably.
ACE Personal Trainer Manual, 5th Edition, p. 409

7. B. Onset of blood lactate accumulation (OBLA)

At high intensities, when the buffering mechanism cannot keep up with the extra acid production, and the pH of the blood begins to fall (due to accumulating lactic acid), the respiratory center is strongly stimulated, and there is an increase in breathing (VT2). This is usually associated with a blood lactate concentration of about 4 mmol/L (this blood lactate concentration is equivalent to the OBLA).
ACE Personal Trainer Manual, 5th Edition, p. 410

8. A. Creating positive experiences and early success through achievable zone 1 exercise of increasing duration

Phase 1 has a principal focus of getting clients who are either sedentary or have little cardiorespiratory fitness to begin engaging in regular cardiorespiratory exercise of low- to moderate-intensity with a primary goal of improving health and a secondary goal of building fitness. The primary goal for the trainer during this phase should be to help the client have positive experiences with cardiorespiratory exercise and to help him or her adopt exercise as a regular habit.
ACE Personal Trainer Manual, 5th Edition, p. 422

9. D. 50

Well-trained and motivated non-athletes can progress to where they are performing as much as 50% of their cardiorespiratory training in zone 2.
ACE Personal Trainer Manual, 5th Edition, p. 427

10. B. Decreasing the number of recovery days per week to accommodate additional interval work

The competitive-level exerciser will need to use a decidedly hard/easy approach to training, or he or she will be at risk for problems from accumulating fatigue and loss of training benefit from the inability to repeatedly do really hard training sessions. Studies have indicated that maladaptations to training (e.g., overtraining syndrome) are almost exclusively attributable to a failure to incorporate appropriate recovery days, particularly if they are coupled with extensive travel or other occupational or social stressors.
ACE Personal Trainer Manual, 5th Edition, p. 429

THE ACE INTEGRATED FITNESS TRAINING® MODEL IN PRACTICE

READING ASSIGNMENT

You should now have completed the reading of Chapter 12 of the *ACE Personal Trainer Manual*, 5th Edition. Carefully review the Summary Review below, as this content highlights valuable information that is particularly relevant to fitness professionals, both in importance and frequency of application or occurrence in the practice of personal training.

Then, answer the Chapter 12 Review Questions and check your answers using the corresponding Answer Key. Review the section in the *ACE Personal Trainer Manual*, 5th Edition, associated with any questions you may have missed.

SUMMARY REVIEW

This chapter presents six case studies featuring the types of clients that many personal trainers will work with on a daily basis in most fitness facilities. This content offers practical examples that should help you synthesize the material presented in Chapters 5 through 11. Each case study provides a scenario in which a personal trainer has to determine a client's current stage of behavioral change, conduct the most effective assessments for the client, and design an exercise program based on the results of the assessments that will also meet the client's goals.

CASE STUDY 1: SHARON

- 33-year-old woman who works from home, has two children under the age of four, and would like to return to her pre-pregnancy fitness level

CASE STUDY 2: DAVID

- 57-year-old business executive and avid recreational athlete who hires a personal trainer to help improve his golf game

CASE STUDY 3: JAN

- 17-year-old female athlete who wants to improve her chances of attaining a volleyball scholarship

CASE STUDY 4: STANLEY

- 28-year-old sedentary male who wants to lose weight and improve his overall health

CASE STUDY 5: MEREDITH

- 64-year-old woman with arthritis who hires a trainer to help her get back in shape and improve her tennis game

CASE STUDY 6: KELLY

- 30-year-old professional woman who wants to lose weight and improve her appearance for her upcoming wedding

GETTING STARTED

The case studies featured in this chapter are designed to enable trainers to identify, develop, and implement programs at the various physiological stages of the ACE Integrated Fitness Training (ACE IFT®) Model. After completing this chapter, you will have a better understanding of:

- How to apply the theoretical knowledge presented in Chapters 5 through 11 in a real-world scenario
- How to interpret assessment results and apply what was learned during the exercise programming process
- How to overcome adherence obstacles when working with clients
- How program modifications can help clients achieve their goals

REVIEW QUESTIONS

**USE THE FOLLOWING CLIENT INFORMATION
TO ANSWER QUESTIONS 1–5:**

Client: Male, age = 38 years

Family history: Father was diagnosed with hypertension at 53 years of age

Smoking: Quit smoking 12 years ago

Height: 70 in (1.78 m)

Weight: 195 lb (88.6 kg)

Body mass index (BMI): 28 kg/m^2

Blood pressure: 137/86 mmHg

Total serum cholesterol: 221 mg/dL

Fasting plasma glucose: 98 mg/dL

Current exercise: Resistance training 60 to 90 minutes per day for the past 7 years, following a five day per week split routine consisting of: chest/shoulders/triceps (2 days/week), back/biceps/core (2 days/week), and legs (1 day/week); warm-up consisting of 10 minutes on the elliptical machine (moderate pace), and cool-down consisting of 5 minutes of stretching for hamstrings

Goals: Recently told by his physician that he is prehypertensive and needs to reduce his total cholesterol. He is worried about having high blood pressure like his father and does not want to go on medication for cholesterol. He would also like to lose about 10 lb (4.5 kg) of body fat while increasing his muscular strength and size. He is planning to train with you two sessions per week for 12 weeks to start.

Initial assessment results:

- Postural screen revealed internal rotation of the shoulders and lordosis

- Movement and flexibility assessments revealed lack of range of motion (ROM) in shoulder external rotation and flexion, a lack of ROM in hip flexion (passive straight-leg raise), and lack of ROM and extension of lumbar spine during the Thomas test

- Trunk endurance tests: Flexion = 80 seconds; extension = 50 seconds; right-side bridge = 50 seconds; left-side bridge = 48 seconds

1. According to the ACSM risk stratification, what is this client's level of risk?
   - A. Low risk
   - B. Moderate risk
   - C. High risk
   - D. Very high risk

2. Based on the ACE IFT Model, what cardiorespiratory assessment would be **MOST** appropriate for this client at this time?
   - A. Submaximal talk test for VT1
   - B. Rockport fitness walking test
   - C. No assessment necessary at this time
   - D. VT2 threshold test

3. Based on this client's current exercise and fitness, what would be the **MOST** appropriate initial cardiorespiratory program to help him work toward his goals?
   - A. Extend warm-up to 15 minutes of steady-state exercise in zone 1, progressively increase duration to 20–30 continuous minutes in zone 1, and then progress to phase 2: aerobic-efficiency training
   - B. Begin with cardiorespiratory programming in phase 2: aerobic-efficiency training, with a primary focus on progressing from low-zone 2 intervals to high-zone 2 intervals to boost caloric expenditure
   - C. Increase to 20 minutes of continuous zone 1 exercise with brief 1-minute intervals (1:3 work-to-recovery intervals). Progress duration to 30 minutes while increasing interval length, and then progress to phase 2: aerobic-efficiency training
   - D. Extend warm-up to 15 minutes, with a 5-minute zone 2 interval in the middle and add a 10-minute cool-down with intensity in zone 1 to increase cardiorespiratory training time to boost caloric expenditure

4. Based on this client's trunk endurance test results, in which of the following ratios did his performance meet the criteria for balanced endurance among the muscle groups tested?
   - A. Flexion:extension ratio
   - B. Right-side bridge:left-side bridge ratio
   - C. Right-side bridge:extension ratio
   - D. Left-side bridge:extension ratio

5. Based on the information provided, what would be the **MOST** appropriate initial functional movement and resistance-training program for this client?

    A. Progress current program using an undulating periodization model, and add a dynamic warm-up to improve core stability

    B. Train proper techniques for squatting, lunging, pushing, pulling, and rotation through movement training (phase 2)

    C. Implement a new load training (phase 3) split routine with an expanded flexibility focus during the cool-down

    D. Work on postural stability, core strength and function, and flexibility through stability and mobility training (phase 1)

USE THE FOLLOWING CLIENT INFORMATION TO ANSWER QUESTIONS 6–10:

Client: Female, age = 27 years

Family history: Mother has osteoporosis; father had coronary bypass surgery at age 52

Smoking: Non-smoker

Height: 64 in (1.63 m)

Weight: 122 lb (55.5 kg)

Body mass index (BMI): 21 kg/m²

Blood pressure: 114/68 mmHg

Total serum cholesterol: 168 mg/dL

Low-density lipoprotein (LDL) cholesterol: 95 mg/dL

High-density lipoprotein (HDL) cholesterol: 64 mg/dL

Fasting plasma glucose: 87 mg/dL

Current exercise: Runs five days per week, with the following distribution: 30-minute run at lunch on Mondays, Wednesdays, and Fridays; long run of 90 minutes on Saturdays; and 60-minute run with a local running group on Sundays. Warm-up consists of five minutes of yoga sun salutations followed by a five-minute walk. Cool-down consists of five minutes of walking plus 10 minutes of static stretching on weekdays and 20 minutes of static stretching on weekends.

Goals: Wants to begin resistance training to reduce her risk for developing osteoporosis, look more "toned," and increase strength for running and injury prevention. Also would like to improve posture to address the neck and low-back soreness she feels when working extended hours

at the computer. She signs up for two personal-training sessions per week for eight weeks.

Initial assessment results:

- Postural screen revealed kyphosis with slight anterior pelvic tilt

- Movement and flexibility assessments revealed good range of motion in all shoulder movements, hip flexion (passive straight-leg raise), and Thomas test, but limited thoracic mobility. Movement during the bend and lift test was initiated with forward knee movement and she was unable to reach the figure-4 position, as her heels lifted off the ground. Good movement and balance during the hurdle step screen.

- Trunk endurance tests: Flexion = 40 seconds; extension = 60 seconds; right-side bridge = 46 seconds; left-side bridge = 44 seconds

6. According to the ACSM risk stratification, what is this client's "total score" for atherosclerotic cardiovascular disease and associated level of risk?

    A. Total score = 0; low risk

    B. Total score = +1; low risk

    C. Total score = +1; moderate risk

    D. Total score = +2; moderate risk

7. Based on the ACE IFT Model, what cardiorespiratory assessment would be **MOST** appropriate for this client at this time?

    A. Pro agility test

    B. Submaximal talk test for VT1

    C. VT2 threshold test

    D. No assessment necessary at this time

8. Based on this client's trunk endurance test results, in which of the following ratios did her performance fail to meet the criteria for balanced endurance among the muscle groups tested?

    A. Flexion:extension ratio

    B. Right-side bridge:left-side bridge ratio

    C. Right-side bridge:extension ratio

    D. Left-side bridge:extension ratio

9. Based on the information provided, what would be the **MOST** appropriate initial functional movement and resistance-training program for this client?

   A. Recommend a group strength class that she can attend for four weeks to help her build initial muscular endurance before beginning her personal-training sessions

   B. Implement a program designed to improve posture and core strength and function through stability and mobility training (phase 1)

   C. Focus initially on developing proper techniques for squatting, lunging, pushing, pulling, and rotation through movement training (phase 2)

   D. Design an initial load training (phase 3) program with 2 sets of 12–16 repetitions on 6–10 machine-based exercises to build initial strength before progressing to more functional exercise

10. Based on this client's performance during the bend and lift screen, what limitations are **MOST** likely preventing her from correctly performing this screen?

    A. Weak core musculature and tight hamstrings

    B. Gluteal group dominance and tight dorsiflexors

    C. Weak quadriceps and plantarflexors

    D. Quadriceps and hip flexor dominance and tight plantarflexors

ANSWER KEY

1. A. Low risk

He has only 1 risk factor (total serum cholesterol ≥200 mg /dL), which places him in the low-risk category.
ACE Personal Trainer Manual, 5th Edition, p. 120–121

2. C. No assessment necessary at this time

Because this client does not currently perform cardiorespiratory exercise, it will be introduced as a new modality in his program. Thus, he will start with phase 1 cardiorespiratory training wherein no assessment is necessary.
ACE Personal Trainer Manual, 5th Edition, p. 422

3. A. Extend warm-up to 15 minutes of steady-state exercise in zone 1, progressively increase duration to 20–30 continuous minutes in zone 1, and then progress to phase 2: aerobic-efficiency training

Because this client is new to cardiorespiratory exercise, he should start in phase 1 training. He can then progress to phase 2 once he can sustain steady-state cardiorespiratory exercise for 20 to 30 minutes in zone 1 [ratings of perceived exertion (RPE) of 3 to 4] and is comfortable with assessments.
ACE Personal Trainer Manual, 5th Edition, p. 422

4. B. Right-side bridge:left-side bridge ratio

For a good relationship between right and left sides, scores should be no greater than 0.05 from a balanced score of 1.0. The client's scores (right-side bridge = 50 seconds; left-side bridge = 48 seconds) indicate an acceptable score of less than 0.05 from a balanced score of 1.0 (50 seconds/48 seconds = 1.04).
ACE Personal Trainer Manual, 5th Edition, p. 191

5. D. Work on postural stability, core strength and function, and flexibility through stability and mobility training (phase 1)

Since this client's posture, core function, and range of motion are in need of improvement, he should have an initial focus of addressing these issues in phase 1 training.
ACE Personal Trainer Manual, 5th Edition, p. 269–270

6. A. Total score = 0; low risk

This client has a total score of 0 [father had coronary bypass surgery at age 52 (+1) and HDL cholesterol of 64 mg/dL (−1)], which represents a low risk.
ACE Personal Trainer Manual, 5th edition, p. 120–121

7. B. Submaximal talk test for VT1

Since this client has experience in endurance running (between 30 and 90 minutes at a time), it would be most appropriate to administer the submaximal talk test to determine HR at VT1.
ACE Personal Trainer Manual, 5th Edition, p. 422

8. C. Right-side bridge:extension ratio

A good extension ratio should be less than 0.75 from either side. Therefore, this client's right-side bridge:extension ratio fell short [right-side bridge = 46; seconds extension = 60 seconds (46/60 = 0.767)].
ACE Personal Trainer Manual, 5th Edition, p. 191

9. B. Implement a program designed to improve posture and core strength and function through stability and mobility training (phase 1)

Since this client's posture, core function, and range of motion are in need of improvement, the program should have an initial focus of addressing these issues in phase 1 training.
ACE Personal Trainer Manual, 5th Edition, p. 269–270

10. D. Quadriceps and hip flexor dominance and tight plantarflexors

The client's forward excursion of the knees implies quadriceps dominance. This results in loading the quadriceps group during a squat movement. The first 10 to 15 degrees of the downward phase are initiated by driving the tibia forward, creating shearing forces across the knee as the femur slides over the tibia. In this lowered position, the gluteus maximus does not eccentrically load and cannot generate much force during the upward phase. Quadriceps-dominant squatting transfers more pressure into the knees, placing greater loads on the anterior cruciate ligament (ACL). The heels lifting off of the floor indicates a potential tightness in the plantarflexors (lack of dorsiflexion).
ACE Personal Trainer Manual, 5th Edition, p. 168–170

MIND-BODY EXERCISE

 READING ASSIGNMENT

You should now have completed the reading of Chapter 13 of the *ACE Personal Trainer Manual,* 5th Edition. Carefully review the Summary Review below, as this content highlights valuable information that is particularly relevant to fitness professionals, both in importance and frequency of application or occurrence in the practice of personal training.

Then, answer the Chapter 13 Review Questions and check your answers using the corresponding Answer Key. Review the section in the *ACE Personal Trainer Manual,* 5th Edition, associated with any questions you may have missed.

SUMMARY REVIEW

Personal trainers should have a basic understanding of the essential tenets of mind-body exercise, including the following terms and concepts:

- Neurobiological foundations of mind-body exercise
- Roots of contemporary mind-body exercise programs
- Differentiating characteristics of mind-body exercise
- Research-supported outcomes and benefits of mind-body exercise
- Common components of mind-body exercise programs
- Yoga research
- Qigong and tai chi research
- Mind-body exercise modalities and programs
  - ✓ Yoga
  - ✓ Qigong exercise
  - ✓ Tai chi
- Contemporary mind-body exercise programs
  - ✓ Pilates
  - ✓ Alexander technique
  - ✓ Feldenkrais method
  - ✓ Nia
  - ✓ Chiwalking and chirunning
  - ✓ American Indian and Alaskan spiritual dancing

ASSESSING OUTCOMES

A personal trainer should be aware of various methods used to objectively measure the response to mind-body exercise, including the following:

- Quality of life
- Blood pressure
- Pulmonary function
- Balance control
- Anxiety and tension
- Spirituality

INDICATIONS FOR MIND-BODY EXERCISE

Personal trainers can utilize a number of common indications for recommending mind-body exercise for their clients, including the following:

- Mind-body exercise and chronic disease management
- Mind-body modalities and acute coronary syndromes

GETTING STARTED

This chapter reviews many of the popular forms of mind-body exercise, both classical and contemporary, and offers practical suggestions for how trainers can incorporate mind-body techniques into training sessions. It also explains the research-supported outcomes and benefits of mind-body exercise. After completing this chapter, you will have a better understanding of:

- The neurological foundations of mind-body exercise
- The classical forms of mind-body exercise—yoga, tai chi, and qigong
- The roots of contemporary forms of mind-body exercise, including Pilates and Nia
- The role of mind-body exercise in chronic disease management
- The general precautions associated with each of these types of exercise

REVIEW QUESTIONS

1. Which of the following benefits of regular participation in mind-body exercise will have the **GREATEST** impact on improved program adherence?
   A. Increased self-efficacy
   B. Enhanced flexibility
   C. Improved muscular strength
   D. Enhanced balance

2. The affective and neuroendocrine response to mind-body exercise is mediated through the hypothalamic-pituitary-adrenal axis (HPA) and results in a decreased production of which hormones that are associated with stress?
   A. Renin and ghrelin
   B. Insulin and glucagon
   C. Catecholamines and cortisol
   D. Serotonin and acetylcholine

3. Which of the following is considered a classical form of mind-body exercise (>200-year heritage)?
   A. Tae kwon do
   B. Pilates
   C. Hatha yoga
   D. Feldenkrais method

4. What is a metabolic benefit of practicing yoga and tai chi on a regular basis?
   A. Increased glucose tolerance and insulin sensitivity
   B. Decreased stress hormones
   C. Increased maximal oxygen uptake
   D. Decreased resting oxygen uptake

5. What is frequently cited as the primary centering activity of mind-body exercise programs?
   A. Breathwork
   B. Kinesthetic awareness
   C. Proper choreographic form
   D. Energycentric movement

6. What is the **PRIMARY** method for progressing the principal challenge in hatha yoga?
   A. Adding an environmental challenge, such as heat
   B. Incorporating a yoga block into the patterns
   C. Adding weighted or external resistance
   D. Increasing the complexity of the asanas

7. Which of the following program modifications would be **MOST** important when teaching yoga to a client who is deconditioned or has a chronic disease?
   A. Increase breath suspensions at the end of expiration to 4–5 seconds
   B. Minimize poses with the head below the heart
   C. Avoid slow transitions from one pose to the next
   D. Increase time holding Iyengar poses for clients with hypertension

8. Which form of mind-body exercise is fundamentally a form of movement re-education that breaks inefficient movement patterns into components?
   A. Iyengar yoga
   B. Tai chi
   C. Qigong
   D. Pilates

9. Which of the following is a characteristic of mind-body exercise programs that is helpful to those with stable chronic disease?
   A. Increased real-time cognitive arousal
   B. Improved proprioception and kinesthesis
   C. Intensity levels ranging from 3–6 METs
   D. Improved aerobic power

10. How can a personal trainer **MOST** effectively incorporate mind-body exercise into personal-training sessions for clients?
    A. Including some Iyengar poses and yogic-breathing during the cool-down
    B. Enhancing power training through slow, controlled yogic breathing
    C. Adding yogic breathing to high-intensity intervals to facilitate greater minute ventilation ($\dot{V}_E$)
    D. Incorporating inverted poses as part of a comprehensive warm-up

ANSWER KEY

1. A. Increased self-efficacy

Regular participation in mind-body exercise has been associated with improved muscular strength, flexibility, balance, and coordination, but perhaps most importantly from a health promotion viewpoint, increased mental development and self-efficacy.
ACE Personal Trainer Manual, 5th Edition, p. 481

2. C. Catecholamines and cortisol

Two key hormones of behavior [corticotropin releasing hormone (CRH) and adrenocorticotropin hormone (ACTH)] inextricably bond brain (hypothalamus and higher brain centers) and body (pituitary and adrenal glands) together. This results in decreased catecholamine and cortisol production and resultant decreased arousal and hypervigilance.
ACE Personal Trainer Manual, 5th Edition, p. 482

3. C. Hatha yoga

Tai chi chuan, qigong exercise, hatha yoga, spiritual and ethnic dance, and some ancient martial arts (e.g., karate, judo, and aikido) all have a heritage older than 200 years.
ACE Personal Trainer Manual, 5th Edition, p. 481

4. A. Increased glucose tolerance and insulin sensitivity

Increased glucose tolerance and insulin sensitivity has been shown in research studies to be a metabolic benefit of regularly practicing yoga and tai chi.
ACE Personal Trainer Manual, 5th Edition, p. 485

5. A. Breathwork

The breath is frequently cited as the primary centering activity in mind-body exercise. There are many breath-centering techniques in yoga, tai chi, and qigong exercise.
ACE Personal Trainer Manual, 5th Edition, p. 486

6. D. Increasing the complexity of the asanas

The principal challenge of hatha yoga is to become proficient at handling increasingly greater amounts of "resistance" (i.e., complexity and the degree of difficulty) in the various asanas and breathing patterns while maintaining a steady and comfortable equilibrium of mind and body.
ACE Personal Trainer Manual, 5th Edition, p. 489

7. B. Minimize poses with the head below the heart

In most cases, those who are initially deconditioned or have a chronic disease should: (a) minimize acute rapid changes in body position (e.g., changes in the limbs and trunk in relation to the heart) in early stages of hatha yoga training, and/or (b) use slower transitions from one yoga pose to the next.
ACE Personal Trainer Manual, 5th Edition, p. 493

8. D. Pilates

Fundamentally, Pilates is a form of movement re-education in which the exerciser learns to overcome faulty compensatory movement patterns.
ACE Personal Trainer Manual, 5th Edition, p. 497

9. B. Improved proprioception and kinesthesis

Characteristics of mind-body exercise programs that are helpful for those with stable chronic disease include the following:
- Can be taught at a relatively low-intensity level (e.g., 2–4 METs) and can be individualized
- Decrease real-time cognitive arousal and stress hormone activation
- Enhance proprioception (muscle sense) and kinesthesis
- Can improve muscular strength, posture, and balance
- Can improve self-efficacy and confidence

ACE Personal Trainer Manual, 5th Edition, p. 500

10. A. Including some Iyengar poses and yogic-breathing during the cool-down

Personal trainers can incorporate any of the select yoga asanas described in the restorative or Iyengar tradition into the flexibility and strength-training components of the program. Further, meditation and yogic-breathing exercises can be integrated with existing warm-up and cool-down exercises.
ACE Personal Trainer Manual, 5th Edition, p. 502

CHAPTER 14

EXERCISE AND SPECIAL POPULATIONS

 READING ASSIGNMENT

You should now have completed the reading of Chapter 14 of the *ACE Personal Trainer Manual*, 5th Edition. Carefully review the Summary Review below, as this content highlights valuable information that is particularly relevant to fitness professionals, both in importance and frequency of application or occurrence in the practice of personal training.

Then, answer the Chapter 14 Review Questions and check your answers using the corresponding Answer Key. Review the section in the *ACE Personal Trainer Manual*, 5th Edition, associated with any questions you may have missed.

SUMMARY REVIEW

An ACE Certified Personal Trainer can work with clients who have health challenges after the clients have been cleared for exercise by their personal physicians. A personal trainer who works with clients with special needs has a responsibility to expand his or her knowledge and skills in this area through continuing education and communication with healthcare professionals.

CARDIOVASCULAR DISORDERS

A personal trainer should understand the general characteristics of coronary artery disease (CAD), including the contributions of the following factors:

- Atherosclerosis
- Dyslipidemia
- Physical inactivity

Exercise and Coronary Artery Disease

An understanding of the following concepts as they relate to exercise and CAD is important for safe and effective exercise programming:

- The role of exercise in the treatment and prevention of CAD
- Mortality and morbidity among patients with CAD
- CAD risk factors

HYPERTENSION

A personal trainer should understand the general characteristics of hypertension, including the contributions of the following factors:

- Age
- Prehypertension
- Diet
- Physical activity
- Antihypertensive medications

Exercise and Hypertension

An understanding of the following concepts as they relate to exercise and hypertension is important for safe and effective exercise programming:

- The role of exercise in the treatment and prevention of hypertension
- Average reduction in blood pressure due to regular exercise
- Magnitude of post-exercise hypotension (PEH)

STROKE

A personal trainer should understand the general characteristics of stroke, including the following:
- Types of stroke (i.e., ischemic and hemorrhagic)
- Risk factors for stroke
- Disability after a stroke
- Warning signs of stroke.

Exercise and Stroke

An understanding of the following concepts as they relate to exercise and stroke is important for safe and effective exercise programming:
- The role of exercise in the treatment and prevention of stroke
- Impact of exercise in cardiovascular disease risk for stroke patients

PERIPHERAL VASCULAR DISEASE

A personal trainer should understand the general characteristics of peripheral vascular disease (PVD):
- Risk factors for PVD
- Peripheral artery occlusive disease (POAD)
- Peripheral vascular occlusive disease (PVOD)
- Claudication pain and the use of the subjective grading scale for PVD

Exercise and Peripheral Vascular Disease

An understanding of the following concepts as they relate to exercise and PVD is important for safe and effective exercise programming:
- The role of exercise in the treatment and prevention of PVD
- Impact of exercise in cardiovascular disease risk for PVD patients

DYSLIPIDEMIA

A personal trainer should understand the general characteristics of dyslipidemia, including the contributions of the following factors:
- Primary lipoproteins
  - ✓ Low-density lipoprotein (LDL)
  - ✓ Very low-density lipoprotein (VLDL)
  - ✓ High-density lipoprotein (HDL)
  - ✓ Non-HDL cholesterol (non-HDL)
- Triglycerides
- 2002 National Cholesterol Education Program (NCEP) Adult Treatment Panel III (ATP III) Classification of LDL, total cholesterol, HDL cholesterol, and triglycerides
- Diet

Exercise and Dyslipidemia

An understanding of the following concepts as they relate to exercise and dyslipidemia is important for safe and effective exercise programming:
- The role of exercise in the treatment and prevention of dyslipidemia
- Average reduction in LDL and increase in HDL due to regular exercise
- The impact of body-fat decrease in the role of lipid profile improvement

DIABETES

A personal trainer should understand the general characteristics of diabetes:
- High levels of blood glucose resulting from defects in insulin production, insulin action, or both
- Manifestations of diabetes (i.e., type 1, type 2, and gestational)
- Chronic health problems associated with diabetes
- Signs and symptoms of type 1 diabetes compared with type 2 diabetes
- Benefits of exercise for individuals with type 1 diabetes
- Benefits of exercise for individuals with type 2 diabetes

METABOLIC SYNDROME

A personal trainer should understand the general characteristics of metabolic syndrome:
- The cluster of conditions that constitute the criteria for metabolic syndrome
- Lifestyle interventions recommended as initial strategies for the treatment of metabolic syndrome

Exercise and the Metabolic Syndrome

An understanding of the following concepts as they relate to exercise and the metabolic syndrome is important for safe and effective exercise programming:
- The role of exercise in the treatment and prevention of the metabolic syndrome
- The impact of obesity on the performance of exercise for individuals with the metabolic syndrome

ASTHMA

A personal trainer should understand the general characteristics of asthma:
- Triggers and symptoms of asthma
- Exercise-induced asthma (EIA)

Exercise and Asthma

An understanding of the following concepts as they relate to exercise and asthma is important for safe and effective exercise programming:
- The role of exercise in the prevention and treatment of asthma
- Medications used to prevent and treat asthma
- Hyperventilation

CANCER

A personal trainer should understand the general characteristics of cancer:
- Influence of age, continued population growth, and improvement in detection technology on future cancer rates
- Malignant and benign tumors
- Metastasis

Exercise and Cancer

An understanding of the following concepts as they relate to exercise and cancer is important for safe and effective exercise programming:
- The role of exercise in the prevention of certain cancers
- The role of exercise in the treatment of cancer
- The impact of chemotherapy and/or radiation treatment on exercise performance

OSTEOPOROSIS

A personal trainer should understand the general characteristics of osteoporosis:
- Common fracture sites and the consequences of those fractures
- Osteopenia
- Bone remodeling
- Impact of lifestyle choices related to bone density

Exercise and Osteoporosis

An understanding of the following concepts as they relate to exercise and osteoporosis is important for safe and effective exercise programming:
- The role of exercise in the prevention and treatment of osteoporosis
- The importance of adequate nutrition in combination with exercise for the treatment of osteoporosis

ARTHRITIS

A personal trainer should understand the general characteristics of arthritis:
- The two primary forms of arthritis (i.e., osteoarthritis and rheumatoid arthritis)
- American College of Rheumatology Revised Criteria for Classification of Functional Status in Rheumatoid Arthritis

Exercise and Arthritis

An understanding of the following concepts as they relate to exercise and arthritis is important for safe and effective exercise programming:
- The role of exercise in the prevention and treatment of arthritis
- The impact of physical inactivity in clients with arthritis

FIBROMYALGIA

A personal trainer should understand the general characteristics of fibromyalgia:
- Common fibromyalgia triggers and symptoms
- 1990 American College of Rheumatology criteria for the diagnosis of fibromyalgia
- Typical treatment modalities for fibromyalgia

Exercise and Fibromyalgia

An understanding of the following concepts as they relate to exercise and fibromyalgia is important for safe and effective exercise programming:
- The role of exercise in the treatment of fibromyalgia
- The impact of physical inactivity in clients with fibromyalgia

CHRONIC FATIGUE SYNDROME

A personal trainer should understand the general characteristics of chronic fatigue syndrome (CFS):
- Common symptoms of CFS
- CFS criteria
- General treatment guidelines for CFS

Exercise Guidelines

A personal trainer should have knowledge of the following concepts related to exercise programming for clients with CFS:
- The role of exercise in the treatment of CFS
- The importance of appropriate rest following physical exertion
- Training approach if exercise worsens CFS symptoms
- Exercise recommendations for clients with CFS

LOW-BACK PAIN

A personal trainer should understand the general characteristics of low-back pain (LBP):
- Prevalence of LBP
- Typical causes of LBP

Exercise and Low-back Pain

An understanding of the following concept as it relates to exercise and LBP is important for safe and effective exercise programming:
- The role of exercise in the prevention and treatment of LBP

WEIGHT MANAGEMENT

A personal trainer should understand the general characteristics of lifestyle modification for weight management:

- Health consequences of overweight and obesity
- Lifestyle habits and cultural changes that contribute to weight gain and obesity

Exercise and Weight Management

An understanding of the following concept as it relates to exercise and weight management is important for safe and effective exercise programming:

- The role of exercise in the prevention and treatment of overweight and obesity

EXERCISE AND OLDER ADULTS

A personal trainer should understand the unique issues related to exercise and older adults, including the contributions of the following factors:

- Normal age-related changes of the cardiovascular, endocrine, respiratory, musculoskeletal, and sensory systems
- The impact of physical activity on the cognitive declines associated with aging

Exercise Guidelines

A personal trainer should have knowledge of the following concepts related to exercise programming for older clients:

- The role of exercise in delaying the physiological declines associated with aging
- The importance of exercises intended to maintain or improve balance
- The impact of physical activity on common chronic health problems experienced by older adults
- Exercise recommendations for older adults

EXERCISE AND YOUTH

A personal trainer should understand the unique issues related to exercise and youth:

- Prevalence and health consequences of physical inactivity among youth
- Health consequences related to poor nutrition habits among youth

Exercise Guidelines

A personal trainer should have knowledge of the following concepts related to exercise programming for youth:

- The health benefits associated with regular physical activity in youth
- Guidelines to minimize the risk of injury during resistance training in youth
- The impact of environmental temperature extremes in exercising youth
- Guidelines for working effectively with youth at different stages of physical and psychological development
- Exercise recommendations for youth

PRE- AND POSTPARTUM EXERCISE

A personal trainer should understand the unique issues related to exercise and the prenatal and postpartum client:

- Evidence in support of the safety of exercise and physical activity during pregnancy and the postpartum period
- Common physiological changes during pregnancy that affect a woman's ability to exercise

Exercise Guidelines for Pregnant Women

A personal trainer should have knowledge of the following concepts related to exercise programming for pregnant clients:

- Published guidelines for exercise during pregnancy and the postpartum period
- Health conditions that preclude pregnant women from exercising
- Contraindicated exercises for pregnant women
- Abnormal signs or symptoms that necessitate delaying or terminating the exercise session
- Exercise recommendations for pregnancy and the postpartum period

GETTING STARTED

This chapter describes a variety of client health concerns that a personal trainer is likely to encounter, and provides exercise guidelines and a sample exercise recommendation for each. Guidelines for working with youth, older adults, and pregnant women are also discussed. After completing this chapter, you will have a better understanding of:

- The following diseases and disorders: coronary artery disease, hypertension, stroke, peripheral vascular disease, dyslipidemia, diabetes, metabolic syndrome, asthma, cancer, osteoporosis, arthritis, fibromyalgia, chronic fatigue syndrome, low-back pain, and overweight and obesity
- The prevalence of each disease or disorder
- How the body's response to exercise is affected by each disease or disorder
- Specific contraindications for exercise associated with each disease or disorder
- Exercise and its role in health for youth, older adults, and pregnant and postpartum women

REVIEW QUESTIONS

1. You are working with a client who has osteoarthritis. He shows up to his latest session and tells you that he has been experiencing soreness in his right knee since helping his daughter move into a new apartment over the weekend. In which section of this client's SOAP notes should this information be recorded?
   A. Subjective
   B. Objective
   C. Assessment
   D. Plan

2. You are working with a client who has hypertension and has been cleared by her physician for exercise. Which of the following would be **MOST** appropriate for her initial resistance-training program?
   A. Mostly body-weight exercises with isometric contractions held initially for 10–15 seconds, working up to 30 seconds
   B. Two sets of 8–12 repetitions on 8–10 exercises addressing all major muscle groups using mostly cables and dumbbells at an intensity of 70–80% 1-RM
   C. One set of 6–8 repetitions performed on 8–10 selectorized machines to address all major muscle groups at an intensity of 80–85% 1-RM
   D. Circuit training consisting of 8–10 exercises using mostly tubing and body weight performed one time for 12–16 repetitions at 60–70% 1-RM

3. What effect does regular exercise have on dyslipidemia?
   A. Exercise alone will significantly reduce total cholesterol levels
   B. Regular exercise can increase LDL levels
   C. Triglyceride levels are reduced for up to 12 hours following exercise
   D. Regular exercise can reduce LDL levels

4. You are working with a client who has type 1 diabetes and checks his blood glucose levels prior to each exercise session. Which of the following pre-exercise blood glucose levels would make you postpone the exercise session until his blood sugar is under control?
   A. 88 mg/dL
   B. 110 mg/dL
   C. 155 mg/dL
   D. 215 mg/dL

5. You are designing an exercise program for a new client who has type 2 diabetes and a physician's release for exercise as tolerated to lose weight and improve blood glucose regulation. During the initial session, you learn that she has been sedentary for the past few years. What initial cardiorespiratory program would be most appropriate for her?
   A. Walking 5–6 days per week for 40 minutes at an RPE of 11–13, working up to 60 minutes
   B. Cycling 3–4 days per week for 40 minutes at an RPE of 13–15, working up to 60 minutes
   C. Walking 5–6 days per week for 10–20 minutes at an RPE of 11–13, working up to 40–60 minutes
   D. Cycling 3–4 days per week for 10–20 minutes at an RPE of 13–15, working up to 40–60 minutes

6. Which of the clients described below meets the criteria for the metabolic syndrome?
   A. 33-year-old male:
      Waist circumference = 36 in (91.4 cm)
      Triglycerides = 188 mg/dL
      HDL cholesterol = 43 mg/dL
      Blood pressure = 130/82 mmHg
      Fasting blood glucose = 95 mg/dL
   B. 42-year-old female:
      Waist circumference = 36 in (91.4 cm)
      Triglycerides = 133 mg/dL
      HDL cholesterol = 47 mg/dL
      Blood pressure = 128/87 mmHg
      Fasting blood glucose = 107 mg/dL
   C. 48-year-old male:
      Waist circumference = 43 in (109.2 cm)
      Triglycerides = 125 mg/dL
      HDL cholesterol = 44 mg/dL
      Blood pressure = 137/88 mmHg
      Fasting blood glucose = 91 mg/dL
   D. 51-year-old female:
      Waist circumference = 33 in (83.8 cm)
      Triglycerides = 172 mg/dL
      HDL cholesterol = 54 mg/dL
      Blood pressure = 127/79 mmHg
      Fasting blood glucose = 98 mg/dL

7. Which of the following steps would be **MOST** appropriate for personal trainers to take to reduce the risk of exercise-induced asthma (EIA) episodes when working with clients who have asthma?

    A. Have clients with asthma use additional inhaler medication prior to all exercise sessions

    B. Keep exercise intensities low-to-moderate for all clients with asthma

    C. Include an extended warm-up and cool-down

    D. Perform exercise sessions outside on hot, dry days

8. Which of the following repetition ranges is recommended to stimulate bone changes in clients who have osteopenia and/or osteoporosis?

    A. 6–8

    B. 10–12

    C. 12–16

    D. 15–20

9. Which of the following progressions is **LEAST** appropriate for clients who have osteoarthritis?

    A. Emphasizing body alignment and exercise techniques at all times

    B. Increasing the weight lifted instead of increasing the number of repetitions

    C. Utilizing a variety of low-impact activities to avoid overstressing the joints

    D. Increasing exercise duration instead of increasing exercise intensity

10. Which of the following statements is **MOST** accurate regarding exercise for people who have low-back pain?

    A. Developing low-back strength is more important for long-term back health than developing low-back endurance.

    B. Low-back exercises have the most beneficial effect when performed on a daily basis.

    C. Full-ROM spinal movements with an external load are best performed shortly after rising from bed.

    D. Supine double-leg raises should be avoided, but prone double-leg raises are beneficial for clients who have low-back pain.

ANSWER KEY

1. A. Subjective

Subjective observations are those that include the client's own status report, a description of symptoms, challenges with the program, and progress made.
ACE Personal Trainer Manual, 5th Edition, p. 513

2. D. Circuit training consisting of 8–10 exercises using mostly tubing and body weight performed one time for 12–16 repetitions at 60–70% 1-RM

Endurance exercise, such as low-impact aerobics, walking, cycling, using ergometers, and swimming, should be the primary exercise mode. Exercises with a significant isometric component should be avoided. Weight training should feature low resistance and a high number of repetitions, as in a circuit-training program. Mind-body exercise such as yoga and tai chi can be used to provide additional variety and promote strength, flexibility, and relaxation.
ACE Personal Trainer Manual, 5th Edition, p. 519–520

3. D. Regular exercise can reduce LDL levels

Research has demonstrated that exercise interventions among adults with cardiovascular disease may reduce LDL cholesterol by 3.0 to 6.0 mg/dL on average.
ACE Personal Trainer Manual, 5th Edition, p. 524–525

4. A. 88 mg/dL

Blood glucose level should be measured before and after each exercise session. The session should be delayed or postponed if the pre-exercise blood glucose level is below 100 mg/dL.
ACE Personal Trainer Manual, 5th Edition, p. 528

5. C. Walking 5–6 days per week for 10–20 minutes at an RPE of 11–13, working up to 40–60 minutes

The primary goals of exercise for most people with type 2 diabetes are better glucose regulation and weight loss, as 80% of this population is overweight. Aerobic exercise of low to moderate intensities at an RPE of 11 to 16 (6 to 20 scale) for 40 to 60 minutes, five or six days per week, is recommended, depending on the client's overall condition and risk profile. Initially, shorter bouts of 10 minutes may be required.
ACE Personal Trainer Manual, 5th Edition, p. 529

6. B. 42-year-old female:
    Waist circumference = 36 in (91.4 cm)
    Triglycerides = 133 mg/dL
    HDL cholesterol = 47 mg/dL
    Blood pressure = 128/87 mmHg
    Fasting blood glucose = 107 mg/dL

The metabolic syndrome is identified as the presence of three or more of the following:
- Elevated waist circumference: Men ≥40 inches (102 cm); Women ≥35 inches (88 cm)
- Elevated triglycerides: ≥150 mg/dL
- Reduced HDL cholesterol: Men <40 mg/dL; Women <50 mg/dL
- Elevated blood pressure: ≥ 130/85 mmHg
- Elevated fasting blood glucose: ≥100 mg/dL

ACE Personal Trainer Manual, 5th Edition, p. 530

7. C. Include an extended warm-up and cool-down

Since EIA is brought on by hyperventilation, individuals with asthma should be encouraged to undertake gradual and prolonged warm-up and cool-down periods. The prolonged, gradual warm-up period will allow some people to utilize the refractory period to lessen the bronchospastic response during subsequent higher-intensity exercise.
ACE Personal Trainer Manual, 5th Edition, p. 533

8. A. 6–8

Depending on the client's physical condition and medical profile, higher-intensity strength-training exercises [eight-repetition maximum (8-RM)] may derive the most benefit to bone. This is the appropriate repetition range for this type of training
ACE Personal Trainer Manual, 5th Edition, p. 538

9. B. Increasing the weight lifted instead of increasing the number of repetitions

Strength training should focus on increasing the number of repetitions rather than increasing the weight being lifted. Clients can gradually increase repetitions from two or three to 10 to 12.
ACE Personal Trainer Manual, 5th Edition, p. 541

10. B. Low-back exercises have the most beneficial effect when performed on a daily basis

While there is a common belief that exercise sessions should be performed at least three times per week, it appears that low-back exercises have the most beneficial effect when performed daily.
ACE Personal Trainer Manual, 5th Edition, p. 549

COMMON MUSCULOSKELETAL
INJURIES AND IMPLICATIONS FOR EXERCISE

 READING ASSIGNMENT

You should now have completed the reading of Chapter 15 of the *ACE Personal Trainer Manual*, 5th Edition. Carefully review the Summary Review below, as this content highlights valuable information that is particularly relevant to fitness professionals, both in importance and frequency of application or occurrence in the practice of personal training.

Then, answer the Chapter 15 Review Questions and check your answers using the corresponding Answer Key. Review the section in the *ACE Personal Trainer Manual*, 5th Edition, associated with any questions you may have missed.

SUMMARY REVIEW

TYPES OF TISSUE AND COMMON TISSUE INJURIES

Personal trainers should have a basic understanding of the following musculoskeletal injuries and their impact on a client's exercise performance:

- Muscle strains
- Ligament sprains
- Common overuse conditions
- Cartilage damage
- Bone fractures

TISSUE REACTION TO HEALING

A personal trainer should understand the following three phases of systematic healing, as well as the signs and symptoms of inflammation:

- Inflammatory phase
- Fibroblastic/proliferation phase
- Maturation/remodeling phase

MANAGING MUSCULOSKELETAL INJURIES

Personal trainers should have a basic understanding of the following concepts related to musculoskeletal injuries and their impact on a client's exercise performance:

- Pre-existing injuries
- Program modification
- Acute injury management
- Flexibility and musculoskeletal injuries

UPPER-EXTREMITY INJURIES

Personal trainers should have a basic understanding of the signs and symptoms, management, and exercise programming guidelines for the following upper-extremity musculoskeletal injuries and their impact on a client's exercise performance:
- Shoulder strain/sprain
- Rotator cuff injuries
- Elbow tendinitis
- Carpal tunnel syndrome

LOW-BACK PAIN

Personal trainers should have a basic understanding of the following concepts related to low-back pain and their impact on a client's exercise performance:
- Common risk factors associated with low-back pain
- Causes of low-back pain
  - ✓ Mechanical pain
  - ✓ Degenerative disc disease and sciatica

LOWER-EXTREMITY INJURIES

Personal trainers should have a basic understanding of the signs and symptoms, management, and exercise programming guidelines for the following lower-extremity musculoskeletal injuries and their impact on a client's exercise performance:
- Greater trochanteric bursitis
- Iliotibial band syndrome
- Patellofemoral pain syndrome
- Infrapatellar tendinitis
- Shin splints
- Ankle sprains
- Achilles tendinitis
- Plantar fasciitis

RECORD KEEPING

A personal trainer should understand the following principles related to appropriate record keeping for his or her client:
- Obtaining a medical history for each client
- Maintaining an exercise record for each client
- Completing and filing an incident report
- Corresponding with other healthcare professionals

GETTING STARTED

This chapter describes how to develop programs for clients with pre-existing musculoskeletal injuries in order to minimize the risk of further injury. This chapter begins by describing the various types of tissue and tissue injury, before detailing specific injuries of the upper and lower extremities. After completing this chapter, you will have a better understanding of:
- The signs and symptoms of inflammation
- The relationship between flexibility and musculoskeletal injuries
- The following upper-extremity injuries: shoulder strain/sprain, rotator cuff injuries, elbow tendinitis, and carpal tunnel syndrome
- The following lower-extremity injuries: greater trochanteric bursitis, iliotibial band syndrome, patellofemoral pain syndrome, infrapatellar tendinitis, shin splints, ankle sprains, Achilles tendinitis, and plantar fasciitis
- The causes of low-back pain
- The importance of proper and thorough record-keeping procedures

REVIEW QUESTIONS

1. Which of the following would be contraindicated for a client who has an acute hamstring strain?
   A. Educating the client about using RICE as an early intervention strategy
   B. Modifying the workout focusing on the non-injured points of the body
   C. Stretching the hamstrings for up to 60 seconds per stretch
   D. Recommending that the client see a physician if pain persists

2. Where is the scapular plane?
   A. In line with the frontal plane
   B. 30 degrees lateral to the sagittal plane
   C. In line with the sagittal plane
   D. 30 degrees anterior to the frontal plane

3. An inflammation of the wrist extensors near their origin is commonly referred to as
   _____.
   A. Medial epicondylitis
   B. Tennis elbow
   C. Golfer's elbow
   D. Olecranon bursitis

4. Which nerve is commonly compressed due to carpal tunnel syndrome?
   A. Median nerve
   B. Ulnar nerve
   C. Radial nerve
   D. Musculocutaneous nerve

5. Clients returning to exercise following greater trochanteric bursitis should generally avoid
   _____.
   A. Prone exercise positions that press on the anterior superior iliac spines
   B. Stretching the iliotibial (IT) band complex
   C. Side-lying exercise positions that compress the lateral hip
   D. Strengthening the deep hip rotator muscles

6. When working with a client who has a history of iliotibial (IT) band syndrome, which muscle group acting on the hip joint is **MOST** likely to be weak?
   A. Hip flexors
   B. Hip extensors
   C. Hip adductors
   D. Hip abductors

7. Tightness in which of the following structures can be a cause of patellofemoral pain syndrome due to its lateral fascial connections to the patella?
   A. IT band complex
   B. Hamstrings
   C. Peroneus longus
   D. Biceps femoris

8. Stretching which muscles has been shown to help relieve symptoms associated with medial tibial stress syndrome (MTSS) and/or anterior shin splints?
   A. Gastrocnemius, soleus, and peroneal group
   B. Soleus and anterior compartment of the lower leg
   C. Tibialis anterior and plantar fascia
   D. Tibialis posterior and lateral compartment

9. What exercises would be **MOST** important to include for a client who has recovered from Achilles tendinitis and wants to prevent it from returning?
   A. Eccentric strengthening for the calf complex through controlled plantar flexion against gravity and stretching the calf muscles
   B. High-intensity strength training for the calf complex and stretching of the flexor hallucis longus and tibialis posterior
   C. Eccentric strengthening for the calf complex through controlled dorsiflexion against gravity and stretching the calf muscles
   D. Comprehensive stretching and isometric strength-training program for the muscles of the lower limb

10. When working with a client who has a history of plantar fasciitis, it would be **MOST** important to include stretching exercises for the

    _____.

    A. Gastrocnemius, soleus, and plantar fascia

    B. Plantar fascia, peroneus longus, and peroneus brevis

    C. Gastrocnemius, tibialis posterior, and tibialis anterior

    D. Plantar fascia, tibialis anterior, and flexor digitorum longus

11. For proper shoe fit, how much space should be given between the shoe and the end of the longest toe?

    A. ½ inch

    B. 2 centimeters

    C. Width of index finger

    D. Length of thumbnail

ANSWER KEY

1. C. Stretching the hamstrings for up to 60 seconds per stretch

Stretching an acutely injured area is contraindicated and could cause further harm.
ACE Personal Trainer Manual, 5th Edition, p. 578

2. D. 30 degrees anterior to the frontal plane

The scapular plane is where the shoulder is positioned 30 degrees between the sagittal and frontal planes.
ACE Personal Trainer Manual, 5th Edition, p. 580

3. B. Tennis elbow

Lateral epicondylitis, which is commonly called "tennis elbow," is defined as an overuse or repetitive-trauma injury of the wrist extensor muscle tendons near their origin on the lateral epicondyle of the humerus.
ACE Personal Trainer Manual, 5th Edition, p. 581–582

4. A. Median nerve

Carpal tunnel syndrome is the most frequently occurring compression syndrome of the wrist. Repetitive wrist and finger flexion when the flexor tendons are strained results in a narrowing of the carpal tunnel due to inflammation, which eventually compresses the median nerve.
ACE Personal Trainer Manual, 5th Edition, p. 582–583

5. C. Side-lying exercise positions that compress the lateral hip

Clients with greater trochanteric bursitis should avoid side-lying positions that compress the lateral hip, as they may still have tenderness over the affected area.
ACE Personal Trainer Manual, 5th Edition, p. 585

6. D. Hip abductors

A client with IT band syndrome may present with weakness in the hip abductors, iliotibial band shortening, and tenderness throughout the iliotibial band complex
ACE Personal Trainer Manual, 5th Edition, p. 587

7. A. IT band complex

Muscle tightness and length deficits have been associated with PFPS. Tightness in the IT band complex (e.g., gluteals) causes an excessive lateral force to the patella via its fascial connection.
ACE Personal Trainer Manual, 5th Edition, p. 588

8. B. Soleus and anterior compartment of the lower leg

Pain-free stretching of the anterior compartment of the lower leg and the calf muscles, especially the soleus, has been shown to be effective in relieving symptoms related to MTSS.
ACE Personal Trainer Manual, 5th Edition, p. 591

9. C. Eccentric strengthening for the calf complex through controlled dorsiflexion against gravity and stretching the calf muscles

Controlled eccentric strengthening of the calf complex has been shown in the literature to be beneficial for helping relieve symptoms (e.g., heel raises standing on the floor and then progressed to standing with the heels hanging off of the edge of a step). Eccentric exercise may reduce pain and improve strength in the presence of Achilles tendinitis.
ACE Personal Trainer Manual, 5th Edition, p. 594

10. A. Gastrocnemius, soleus, and plantar fascia

Stretching of the gastrocnemius, soleus, and plantar fascia is beneficial and has been shown to help relieve symptoms in the plantar fascia.
ACE Personal Trainer Manual, 5th Edition, p. 596

11. C. Width of index finger

Allow a space up to the width of the index finger between the end of the longest toe and the end of the shoe. This space will accommodate foot size increases, a variety of socks, and foot movement within the shoe without hurting the toes.
ACE Personal Trainer Manual, 5th Edition, p. 586

EMERGENCY PROCEDURES

 READING ASSIGNMENT

You should now have completed the reading of Chapter 16 of the *ACE Personal Trainer Manual,* 5th Edition. Carefully review the Summary Review below, as this content highlights valuable information that is particularly relevant to fitness professionals, both in importance and frequency of application or occurrence in the practice of personal training.

Then, answer the Chapter 16 Review Questions and check your answers using the corresponding Answer Key. Review the section in the *ACE Personal Trainer Manual,* 5th Edition, associated with any questions you may have missed.

SUMMARY REVIEW

Personal trainers should have a systematic approach for handling various types of emergency situations and have knowledge of concepts related to the following emergency-specific factors:

- Personal protective equipment
- Scene safety
- Maintaining a first-aid kit
- Emergency policies and procedures for fitness facilities
- Record keeping and confidentiality
  ✓ Health Insurance Portability and Accountability Act (HIPAA)
- Emergency assessment
- Activating emergency medical services (EMS)
- Initial response
  ✓ Cardiopulmonary resuscitation (CPR)
  ✓ Automated external defibrillation (AED)

COMMON MEDICAL EMERGENCIES AND INJURIES

Personal trainers should have basic knowledge of the following common medical emergencies and injuries, the signs and symptoms of each, and recommended treatments:

- Dyspnea
- Choking
- Asthma
- Cardiovascular disease, chest pain, and heart attack
- Syncope
- Stroke
- Diabetes and insulin reaction (hypoglycemia)
- Heat illness
- Cold illness
- Seizures
- Soft-tissue injuries
- Fractures
- Head injuries
- Neck and back injuries
- Shock

UNIVERSAL PRECAUTIONS AND PROTECTION AGAINST BLOODBORNE PATHOGENS

Due to the threat of communicable disease, personal trainers should understand universal precautions when dealing with bloodborne pathogens, specifically hepatitis B and C and human immunodeficiency virus (HIV).

GETTING STARTED

This chapter describes most of the common medical emergencies that personal trainers might encounter, as well as appropriate procedures for responding to them. After completing this chapter, you will have a better understanding of:

- The various types of emergency equipment and emergency medical services
- The steps for primary and secondary assessment
- The ABCs of basic life support
- The symptoms of common medical emergencies and injuries
- Practices that may prevent medical emergencies
- Bloodborne pathogens and how to avoid exposure
- Cardiopulmonary resuscitation and automated external defibrillation

REVIEW QUESTIONS

1. What is the **MOST** important step a fitness facility can take to minimize risks of cardiovascular events?
   A. Having each member complete a release of liability waiver and informed consent
   B. Requiring all members to have physical examinations before beginning exercise programs
   C. Having each member complete a medical history form
   D. Requiring all members to start programs at a low-to-moderate intensity

2. Which of the following **CORRECTLY** describes the Health Insurance Portability and Accountability Act (HIPAA) of 1996?
   A. It ensures individual privacy by requiring confidentiality of health documents
   B. It requires an individual to share health information with his or her physician
   C. It requires an individual to share health information with his or her insurance agency
   D. It ensures that individual health records are accessible at all times via an electronic database

3. What should you do **FIRST** with a person who suddenly falls to the floor while exercising?
   A. Ask the person what led to the injury
   B. Check for any medical jewelry to determine the cause of the condition
   C. Assess the person's pulse and blood pressure
   D. Assess if the person is conscious and ask if he or she is okay

4. What is the **PRIMARY** reason people give for not attempting CPR in a cardiac emergency?
   A. Fear of lawsuits due to cracked ribs
   B. Uncertainty about their ability to perform CPR correctly
   C. Fear of performing CPR when it is not needed
   D. Uncomfortable with putting their mouth on a stranger

5. What is the **MOST** common heart rhythm during cardiac arrest?
   A. Atrial fibrillation
   B. Atrial bradycardia
   C. Ventricular fibrillation
   D. Ventricular tachycardia

6. A heart attack is characterized by which of the following signs and symptoms?
   A. A sudden, severe headache and weakness on one side of the body
   B. Sustained stabbing pain in and around the chest
   C. Sudden loss of consciousness, with no breathing and no pulse
   D. A squeezing pressure in the chest that can be mistaken for heartburn

7. How is a transient ischemic attack (TIA) different from a stroke?
   A. A TIA is caused by a different physiological mechanism
   B. A stroke is not treatable, but a TIA is
   C. Signs of a TIA last less than one hour
   D. A TIA feels less severe and is less frightening than a stroke

8. Which of the following are actions to take when you suspect a client is having a mild hypoglycemic incident?
   A. Help the client sit down and give him or her a sugary drink if he can swallow
   B. Call EMS rescuers, start the steps of CPR, and get an available AED
   C. Help the client sit down and give insulin if he or she has it available
   D. Immediately call for EMS rescuers to respond and monitor the person

9. Which of the following is a critical indicator that someone is suffering from heat stroke and in need of emergency treatment?
   A. Increased body temperature
   B. Altered mental status
   C. Red hot, sweaty skin
   D. Fatigue, weakness, and headache

10. Which treatment of soft-tissue injuries is within the personal trainer scope of practice?
    A. Recommending that the client take non-steroidal anti-inflammatory drugs (NSAIDs)
    B. Performing massage on the affected soft tissue
    C. Administering ultrasound to the affected soft tissue
    D. Educating the client on the proper administration of ice using the RICE principle

11. Which region of the spine is the most prone to catastrophic injury?
    A. Cervical
    B. Thoracic
    C. Lumbar
    D. Sacrum

ANSWER KEY

1. C. Having each member complete a medical history form

Facilities should screen new members to identify those at high risk for cardiovascular events by using a simple screening questionnaire such as the Physical Activity Readiness Questionnaire (PAR-Q). People with cardiac disease are 10 times more likely to have a cardiovascular event during exercise than those who are apparently healthy. The PAR-Q can help to identify high-risk individuals who need medical referral or require modifications to their exercise programs.
ACE Personal Trainer Manual, 5th Edition, p. 604

2. A. It ensures individual privacy by requiring confidentiality of health documents

The Health Insurance Portability and Accountability Act (HIPAA) of 1996 is a federal law that ensures the victim's privacy by putting him or her in control of who has access to personal health information.
ACE Personal Trainer Manual, 5th Edition, p. 606

3. D. Assess if the person is conscious and ask if he or she is okay

With a conscious victim, the rescuer should introduce him- or herself, ask what the problem is, and ask if he or she can provide any help. (Consent to receive help must be given verbally if the victim is conscious and alert.)
ACE Personal Trainer Manual, 5th Edition, p. 606

4. B. Uncertainty about their ability to perform CPR correctly

Interviews with people who witnessed a cardiac arrest have found that the major reason bystanders do not attempt to perform CPR is because they panic. Although more than half of the interviewees had CPR training at some time in their lives, many reported that they were afraid to cause harm or afraid they would not perform well. The fear of disease was not a factor because most were family members of the victim.
ACE Personal Trainer Manual, 5th Edition, p. 610

5. C. Ventricular fibrillation

During cardiac arrest, the heart is beating erratically and ineffectively. The most common rhythm during cardiac arrest is ventricular fibrillation (VF), which is a spasmodic quivering of the heart that is too fast to allow the heart chambers to adequately fill and empty, so little or no blood is pushed out to the body or lungs.
ACE Personal Trainer Manual, 5th Edition, p. 611

6. D. A squeezing pressure in the chest that can be mistaken for heartburn

A heart attack is due to an obstruction in a coronary vessel that prevents part of the heart muscle from getting adequate blood flow and oxygen. When plaque builds up in the arteries and prevents proper blood flow to the heart, chest pain called angina pectoris can occur. Angina pectoris is described as chest pressure or a squeezing feeling, which may be mistaken for heartburn or indigestion.
ACE Personal Trainer Manual, 5th Edition, p. 614

7. C. Signs of a TIA last less than one hour

A transient ischemic attack (TIA) can mimic the symptoms of a stroke but causes only temporary disability. Symptoms usually last less than one hour and may be relieved within 10 or 15 minutes.
ACE Personal Trainer Manual, 5th Edition, p. 616

8. A. Help the client sit down and give him or her a sugary drink if he can swallow

If the client is conscious and can swallow, he or she should consume 20 to 30 grams of carbohydrates such as a sugary drink (juice or regular soda) or a packet of sugar or honey to raise the blood sugar back to a normal level.
ACE Personal Trainer Manual, 5th Edition, p. 617

9. B. Altered mental status

The signs and symptoms of heat stroke include a change in mental status, such as irritability and aggressiveness, which may progress to apathy, confusion, unresponsiveness, or even coma.
ACE Personal Trainer Manual, 5th Edition, p. 620

10. D. Educating the client on the proper administration of ice using the RICE principle

General primary treatment for soft-tissue injuries is RICE (rest or restricted activity, ice, compression, and elevation). The diagnosis and treatment of injuries is outside the scope of practice of a personal trainer.
ACE Personal Trainer Manual, 5th Edition, p. 625

11. A. Cervical

The uppermost part of the spinal column, the cervical spine, is located in the neck and made up of seven cervical vertebrae. This part of the spinal cord is the most mobile and delicate, and the most likely to become injured.
ACE Personal Trainer Manual, 5th Edition, p. 629

LEGAL GUIDELINES
AND PROFESSIONAL RESPONSIBILITIES

READING ASSIGNMENT

You should now have completed the reading of Chapter 17 of the *ACE Personal Trainer Manual*, 5th Edition. Carefully review the Summary Review below, as this content highlights valuable information that is particularly relevant to fitness professionals, both in importance and frequency of application or occurrence in the practice of personal training.

Then, answer the Chapter 17 Review Questions and check your answers using the corresponding Answer Key. Review the section in the *ACE Personal Trainer Manual*, 5th Edition, associated with any questions you may have missed.

SUMMARY REVIEW

To achieve professional success, personal trainers must have knowledge regarding the following business- and legal-related concepts and their impact on the professional environment:

- Business structure
  - ✓ Sole proprietorships
  - ✓ Partnerships
  - ✓ Corporations
- Independent contractors
- Employees
- Agreements to participate
- Informed consent
- Waivers
- Scope of practice
- Liability insurance
- Legal responsibilities
  - ✓ Facilities
  - ✓ Equipment
  - ✓ Supervision
  - ✓ Instruction
- Other business concerns with legal implications
  - ✓ Marketing activities
  - ✓ Intellectual property
  - ✓ Proper use of the ACE name and logo
  - ✓ Transportation
  - ✓ Financing
- Risk management

GETTING STARTED

This chapter is designed to increase your comfort level with the legal issues related to personal training and address some of the legal and business concerns you may have as a personal trainer. After completing this chapter, you will have a better understanding of:

- The legal responsibilities of a personal trainer
- The differences between independent contractors and employees
- The elements of a binding contract
- The types of business structures available to personal trainers, as well as the advantages and disadvantages of each
- Basic legal concepts and defenses

REVIEW QUESTIONS

1. What business structure puts a personal trainer at the **GREATEST** risk for losing personal assets in the event of a lawsuit filed by a client for an incident related to personal-training services provided?
   A. C-corporation
   B. Sole proprietorship
   C. Limited liability corporation
   D. Subchapter S-corporation

2. Which business structure combines the limited liability and flow-through taxation of the S-corp with easier creation and operation requirements?
   A. Partnership
   B. C-corporation
   C. Limited liability partnership
   D. Sole proprietorship

3. What is a personal trainer **MOST** likely to give up when switching from working as an independent contractor to working as an employee of a fitness facility?
   A. Social security taxes being withheld and matched by the facility
   B. Medical benefits covered by the facility
   C. Need for justification from the facility before being fired
   D. Flexibility to set his or her own schedule and pricing

4. Which of the following business practices would be **MOST** likely to put a facility at risk for improperly categorizing personal trainers as independent contractors?
   A. Allowing independent contractors to set their own schedules
   B. Requiring all personal trainers to follow the same assessment and programming procedures
   C. Allowing independent contractors to set their own fees
   D. Requiring all personal trainers to hold their own professional liability insurance

5. What is the **BEST** method for ensuring that all aspects of a client–personal trainer relationship are properly established?
   A. Signed contract
   B. Informed consent
   C. Liability waiver
   D. Verbal agreement

6. In which scenario is the personal trainer **MOST** likely to be found guilty of negligence?
   A. The trainer suffers a low-back injury while spotting a client
   B. The client gets injured on her way into the fitness facility for her training session
   C. The trainer is talking with another club member while the client injures himself due to poor form
   D. The client follows his program but adds two more sets on all exercises and sustains an injury as a result

7. What is the legal term used to describe a situation where a trainer fails to act and a client is injured, but the client is determined to have played a role in his or her own injury?
   A. Contributory negligence
   B. Gross negligence
   C. Complete negligence
   D. Comparative negligence

8. What form is used to have the client acknowledge that he or she has been specifically informed about the risks associated with the activity in which he or she is about to engage?
   A. Liability waiver
   B. Informed consent
   C. Agreement to participate
   D. Exculpatory clause

9. Personal trainers who provide training sessions to individuals and/or groups in clients' homes or outdoor settings should check with their current insurance providers to see if they are covered for training in these settings or if they need to add a(n) _____ policy to their existing professional liability insurance.
   A. General liability insurance

   B. Keyman insurance

   C. Umbrella insurance

   D. Specific insurance rider

10. Which of the following would violate intellectual property laws?
    A. Using music specifically designed for use in fitness facilities during small-group personal training

    B. ACE Certified Professionals listing their ACE certification on their business cards

    C. Allowing personal-training clients the option to bring their own music to be played during their training sessions

    D. Using the ACE logo to promote nutritional products, DVDs, or equipment sold by an ACE Certified Professional

11. What is the recommended amount of professional liability insurance coverage that personal trainers should carry?
    A. $200,000
    B. $500,000
    C. $1,000,000
    D. $2,000,000

ANSWER KEY

1. B. Sole proprietorship

In a sole proprietorship, financial losses and liabilities are the sole responsibility of the owner. There is no corporate veil that shields the actions of the business from the personal responsibility of the owner, even if the owner conducts business under a different company name. Delinquent debts and successful lawsuits against the business can result in the owner being required to sell personal assets to pay the judgment.
ACE Personal Trainer Manual, 5th Edition, p. 640

2. C. Limited liability partnership

Forming and operating a subchapter S-corporation requires extensive paperwork and attention to detail. For this reason, many small business owners have chosen to operate as LLCs or LLPs. An LLC or LLP operates in many ways like a subchapter S-corporation. Profits flow through to the investors and are taxed as ordinary income. The LLC and LLP also provide a corporate veil against personal liability. However, LLCs and LLPs typically can be established by filing simple paperwork in the state where the LLC/LLP will initially operate.
ACE Personal Trainer Manual, 5th Edition, p. 643

3. D. Flexibility to set his or her own schedule and pricing

Creating schedules, requiring specific materials to be utilized, and overseeing procedures typically indicate an employment relationship.
ACE Personal Trainer Manual, 5th Edition, p. 647

4. B. Requiring all personal trainers to follow the same assessment and programming procedures

Creating schedules, requiring specific materials to be utilized, and overseeing procedures typically indicate an employment relationship.
ACE Personal Trainer Manual, 5th Edition, p. 647

5. A. Signed contract

A signed contract detailing the relationship between the trainer and the client as they pertain to the potential rigors and injuries associated with physical activity, as well the expectations of both parties, is the best method for properly establishing a client–personal trainer relationship.
ACE Personal Trainer Manual, 5th Edition, p. 652

6. C. The trainer is talking with another club member while the client injures himself due to poor form

Failing to perform as a reasonable and prudent person would under similar circumstances is considered negligence. A negligent act can occur if a trainer fails to act (act of omission) or acts inappropriately (act of commission). For example, a trainer could be successfully sued for neglecting to spot a client during a free-weight bench press (omission), or for programming straight-leg sit-ups for a client with known lower-back problems (commission).
ACE Personal Trainer Manual, 5th Edition, p. 649

7. A. Contributory negligence

Courts will typically examine every aspect of the scenario to determine who was at fault. In some cases, the client may have contributed to the potential injury. In certain states, contributory negligence laws prevent a plaintiff in a lawsuit who has played some role in the injury from receiving any remuneration.
ACE Personal Trainer Manual, 5th Edition, p. 652

8. B. Informed consent

An informed consent form can be utilized by a personal trainer to demonstrate that a client acknowledges that he or she has been specifically informed about the risks associated with the activity in which he or she is about to engage.
ACE Personal Trainer Manual, 5th Edition, p. 654

9. D. Specific insurance rider

General liability policies may not cover a personal trainer who works with clients in a private residence. Owners who will use their own home or a client's home should ensure that a specific insurance rider—a special addition to typical policy provisions—will cover those activities.
ACE Personal Trainer Manual, 5th Edition, p. 665

10. D. Using the ACE logo to promote nutritional products, DVDs, or equipment sold by an ACE Certified Professional

ACE Certified Professionals can use the ACE logo mark to promote their credentials to clients. ACE Certified Professionals must not use the American Council on Exercise name or ACE logo on any materials that promote their services as a trainer or instructor of other fitness professionals, such as continuing education courses, seminars, or basic training, unless it is contained within their personal biographical material. In addition, ACE Certified Professionals must not use the American Council on Exercise name or ACE logo in conjunction with any other product or merchandise that they sell, such as videos or clothing.

ACE Personal Trainer Manual, 5th Edition, p. 668

11. C. $1,000,000

ACE recommends retaining at least $1 million in coverage, as medical expenses can easily cost hundreds of thousands of dollars. In some instances, a higher liability coverage amount may be advisable.

ACE Personal Trainer Manual, 5th Edition, p. 664

PERSONAL-TRAINING
BUSINESS FUNDAMENTALS

 READING ASSIGNMENT

You should now have completed the reading of Chapter 18 of the *ACE Personal Trainer Manual*, 5th Edition. Carefully review the Summary Review below, as this content highlights valuable information that is particularly relevant to fitness professionals, both in importance and frequency of application or occurrence in the practice of personal training.

Then, answer the Chapter 18 Review Questions and check your answers using the corresponding Answer Key. Review the section in the *ACE Personal Trainer Manual*, 5th Edition, associated with any questions you may have missed.

SUMMARY REVIEW

A personal trainer should have knowledge of the different business environments that he or she might encounter and their role in overall career development.

THE DIRECT EMPLOYEE MODEL

A personal trainer should consider the following factors when making a decision about whether or not to work for an employer:

- Clientele
- Location of facility
- Reputation of the company
- Requirements for employment
- Production expectations of the company
- The various advantages of working in the direct employee model
- The various disadvantages of working in the direct employee model

THE INDEPENDENT CONTRACTOR MODEL

A personal trainer should consider the following factors when making a decision about whether or not to work as an independent contractor:

- How much to charge for services
- Which facility to use
- The type and amount of operational costs that will be incurred
- Which health-screening forms and legal documents to use
- The various advantages of working as an independent contractor
- The various disadvantages of working as an independent contractor

BUSINESS PLANNING

To have a successful career, a personal trainer should take the time to perform an assessment of his or her own financial fitness and use that information to develop a business plan that includes the following components:
- Executive summary
- Business description
- Marketing plan
- Operational plan
- Risk analysis
  - ✓ SWOT analysis
- Decision-making criteria

CREATING A BRAND

A personal trainer should use the business-planning process to develop a brand identity for his or her training service:
- Conducting market research
- Targeting clientele
- Communicating a unique brand identity
- Creating a personal vision statement

A personal trainer should have the ability to promote, develop, and maintain his or her services by applying concepts related to the following business-related topics:
- Communicating the benefits
- Marketing for client retention
- Marketing through general communication

CHOOSING A BUSINESS STRUCTURE

When starting a business, a personal trainer should consider the following areas of business ownership:
- How to structure the business
- Whether to work with partners
- Whether to establish a corporate structure

PROFESSIONAL SERVICES FOR STARTING A BUSINESS

A personal trainer should consider the services provided by the following professionals when starting a business:
- Attorney
- Accountant
- Web developer/graphic designer
- Insurance broker
- Real estate broker
- Contractors

FINANCIAL PLAN

To be successful, personal trainers should consider establishing budget and revenue goals for themselves:
- Identify expenses
- Identify revenues
- Set income goals
- Identify specific details for how the business will generate cash flow and produce a profit

TIME MANAGEMENT

It is important for personal trainers to develop a schedule that accommodates all of their needs while taking into account the following activities:

- Working with clients
- Client management
- Prospecting for new clients
- Developing marketing or advertising materials
- Other job duties

HOW TO SELL PERSONAL TRAINING

A personal trainer should have an understanding of the following concepts and strategies while selling his or her services:

- Effectively communicating how the knowledge and skills of a personal trainer can meet or exceed the needs of a potential client
- Asking for the sale
- Seven basic rules for selling
- Four basic questions that are required to move from presenting information to closing the sale
- Selling training programs versus selling training sessions

GETTING STARTED

This chapter provides the basics of running a personal-training business, including business planning, marketing, and financial planning. It also explains the advantages and disadvantages of working as an independent contractor or direct employee. After completing this chapter, you will have a better understanding of:

- How to develop a sound business plan
- How to create a brand and communicate the benefits of a business
- Marketing to acquire new clients and retain existing ones
- The professional services needed to run a successful business, including an attorney, accountant, and web developer
- How to sell personal-training services

REVIEW QUESTIONS

1. Which of the following situations would put an independent contractor at risk for prosecution?
   A. Renting training space from a fitness facility
   B. Training in clients' homes using their equipment
   C. Deciding not to train clients at a facility that utilizes practices the trainer feels to be unethical
   D. Training clients for a fee in a facility without notifying or paying the facility owner

2. The mission statement and business model should be detailed in which component of the business plan?
   A. Business description
   B. Operational plan
   C. Executive summary
   D. Marketing plan

3. When conducting a SWOT analysis, where should a personal trainer list the following entry: "The club is unable to meet the needs of the current volume of potential personal-training clientele"?
   A. Strengths
   B. Weaknesses
   C. Opportunities
   D. Threats

4. What is the **BEST** way for a personal trainer to establish relatively immediate emotional connections with clients by defining the quality of personal-training services clients can expect?
   A. Writing a well-detailed business description
   B. Developing a strong brand
   C. Writing a good executive summary
   D. Developing a strong operational plan

5. Which of the following would be the **LEAST** effective method for a personal trainer to attract potential new clients?
   A. Teaching several group exercise classes each week
   B. Offering complimentary monthly talks on timely fitness topics
   C. Posting a trainer profile filled with personal athletic achievements
   D. Leading a free group-training session for a local running event

6. Which of the following would **MOST** likely be seen as a limitation by a client participating in small-group personal training?
   A. Another participant in the group who requires constant individual attention from the trainer
   B. Social support and encouragement received by others in the group
   C. Dissociation from the unpleasant sensations of vigorous exercise due to interaction with others
   D. Personal commitment to adhere to the exercise sessions due to group dynamics

7. In addition to marketing personal-training services to clients, what other skill must a personal trainer develop to become successful at selling training sessions?
   A. Designing good exercise programs
   B. Being able to ask for the sale
   C. Dressing professionally
   D. Maintaining a high level of fitness

8. Which of the following is an example of a question that focuses on the needs of the client?
   A. "What has kept you from achieving your goals in the past?"
   B. "Would you be interested in the camaraderie of small-group personal training sessions?"
   C. "How did you find out about our personal-training services?"
   D. "Would you be interested in the weight-loss training package that we offer?"

9. What is an advantage of selling personal-training programs that have a specific outcome focus such as weight loss or preparation for a specific event?
   A. They increase client motivation because they generally guarantee success
   B. They help weed out clients who are unlikely to commit to a long-term training program
   C. They allow personal trainers to put multiple clients on the same program to save time and effort
   D. They foster program adherence, as clients begin the program with a specific goal in mind

10. Which of the following activities do busy personal trainers often neglect in the day-to-day operations of their business?

    A. Working with clients

    B. Client management

    C. Exercise

    D. Marketing

11. What is the recommended first step for a personal trainer in establishing a personal budget?

    A. List all monthly expenses

    B. List all sources of monthly income

    C. Determine the amount of money to charge per session

    D. Determine the number of training sessions each week

ANSWER KEY

1. D. Training clients for a fee in a facility without notifying or paying the facility owner

The personal trainer must keep in mind that some fitness facilities will prosecute trainers for shoplifting or trespassing if they are caught training "under the table"—being paid directly by a client. Because this practice is illegal and unethical, it violates the ACE Code of Ethics and could lead to the loss of the ACE credential. Training under the table might seem like a tempting option for a beginning or struggling trainer, but there are serious potential consequences.
ACE Personal Trainer Manual, 5th Edition, p. 677

2. A. Business description

The business description portion of the business plan provides the details for the business as outlined in the executive summary, including the mission statement, business model, current status of the market, how the business fills a need within the market, and the management team.
ACE Personal Trainer Manual, 5th Edition, p. 679

3. C. Opportunities

In a SWOT analysis, the items labeled "opportunities" are all of the opportunities for attracting new clients or expanding the business.
ACE Personal Trainer Manual, 5th Edition, p. 681

4. B. Developing a strong brand

A brand represents what a service or product stands for and is an easy way to communicate its value to potential customers and clients. Creating a brand to define the quality of personal-training service that a client can expect is an important step in establishing an almost immediate emotional connection with a client.
ACE Personal Trainer Manual, 5th Edition, p. 682

5. C. Posting a trainer profile filled with personal athletic achievements

Attracting clients involves connecting with them and describing how you can help them reach their goals. Promoting your own athletic achievements does little to spread that message.
ACE Personal Trainer Manual, 5th Edition, p. 684–685

6. A. Another participant in the group who requires constant individual attention from the trainer
Clients who require constant individual attention are a definite limitation to small-group training sessions.
ACE Personal Trainer Manual, 5th Edition, p. 689–691

7. B. Being able to ask for the sale

The sales process requires asking someone—a prospective client—to make a commitment to his or her personal fitness goals by investing in the personal trainer through the purchase of training sessions.
ACE Personal Trainer Manual, 5th Edition, p. 700–701

8. A. "What has kept you from achieving your goals in the past?"

The sales conversation should focus on what the client needs and wants, as well as on how the trainer can help. The following questions focus on the needs of the client:
- You have told me your goals. How long have you had these goals?
- Why is it so important that you achieve these goals?
- What has kept you from achieving these goals in the past?
- From what you have told me, I think I can help you work toward meeting these goals. Would you like that?
ACE Personal Trainer Manual, 5th Edition, p. 703

9. D. They foster program adherence, as clients begin the program with a specific goal in mind

A benefit of a defined-outcome training program is that it can help the client adhere to an exercise routine, because he or she is able to begin the program with a specific end in mind.
ACE Personal Trainer Manual, 5th Edition, p. 704–705

10. C. Exercise

An important part of being a personal trainer is maintaining a healthy lifestyle and serving as a role model, which includes following an exercise program. It is not uncommon for new trainers to become so busy with clients that they fail to make time for their own workouts.
ACE Personal Trainer Manual, 5th Edition, p. 699

11. A. List all monthly expenses

The first step to take when establishing a personal budget is to list monthly expenses. The trainer should identify all categories of fixed costs, such as rent, transportation, and utilities, as well as variable costs such as food, entertainment, and professional development.
ACE Personal Trainer Manual, 5th Edition, p. 695

APPENDIX

CERTIFICATION
INFORMATION GUIDE

I. PURPOSE

The purpose of this information is to provide you with insight into the American Council on Exercise's (ACE) certification process. By understanding how the examination is developed, we believe you can better prepare for the exam. ACE follows the highest standards for professional and occupational certification tests, taking measures to uphold validity, reliability, and fairness for all candidates in our examinations.

II. HOW IS THE EXAM DEVELOPED?

ACE certification examinations are developed by ACE and volunteer committees of subject matter experts in the field(s) in cooperation with Castle Worldwide, Inc., an independent testing agency. The exam development process involves the following steps:

A. Job Analysis

A committee of experts in the health and fitness field thoroughly analyzes the job requirements (tasks) and develops an outline of the knowledge and skills necessary to perform the job competently.

B. Validation Study

A research survey is then conducted to determine if the job analysis is valid. This survey is sent to thousands of randomly selected fitness professionals who currently hold the certification for input and validation. The final outcome is the Exam Content Outline (see Appendix B in the *ACE Personal Trainer Manual*).

C. Item Writing

A national panel of experts develops questions for the exam. Questions are tied specifically to the validated Exam Content Outline, which resulted from the job analysis. All questions are also referenced to an acceptable text or document and further validated for importance, criticality, and relevance. Castle then reviews and edits the questions to ensure that they adhere to certification-industry best practices.

D. Exam Construction

The questions are then reviewed in detail one more time by the examination committee before being placed on the final exam forms. New questions are first introduced as experimental items to see if they perform statistically well before being introduced as scored items that impact a candidate's actual score.

E. Cut Score Determination

Once the final exam is constructed, the exam committee rates the difficulty of each question and the passing point is then determined by statistical analysis of the committee ratings. This analysis adjusts for variability in the ratings and gives benefit to the test candidate.

F. Continual Exam Evaluation

Once the exam process is completed, continual evaluation and analysis of each question helps to ensure validity. Multiple test forms are produced each year, with the passing point equated to the cut score of the original form to ensure an equivalent passing point across all test forms for the certification program. Approximately every five years the exam-development process begins again with a new job analysis.

III. HOW IS THE EXAM ADMINISTERED?

An independent testing agency is used to administer all ACE examinations to ensure exam security, integrity, and the elimination of bias. Be assured that all of the policies that ACE follows concerning exam administration are required to maintain these high standards and accreditation from the National Commission for Certifying Agencies (NCCA).

IV. WHO IS ELIGIBLE TO TAKE THE EXAM?

Anyone who is at least 18 years of age, has a high school diploma or equivalent, and has a valid CPR and AED certification that includes a live skills check is eligible to take the ACE Personal Trainer Certification Exam. For the ACE Personal Trainer Certification Examination it is assumed that the examinee will be competent in the areas described in the Exam Content Outline found in Appendix B of the *ACE Personal Trainer Manual.* Please visit the ACE website (www.ACEfitness.org) for information concerning fees, registration procedures, and testing dates and sites.